Seasons
OUT OF TIME

JACKSON KING

Tellwell Talent
www.tellwell.ca

ISBN
978-0-2288-0161-0 (Paperback)
978-0-2288-0162-7 (eBook)

SEASONS OUT OF TIME

"We had seasons in the sun
But the hills that we climbed
Were just seasons out of time."

Seasons in the Sun
(Sung by Terry Jacks;
Music and original lyrics by Jacques Brel;
English lyrics by Rod McKuen)

"Only through experience of trial and suffering
can the soul be strengthened, vision cleared,
ambition inspired, and success achieved."

Helen Keller

Dedication

To God in heaven, my lifelong companion, who
believed in me when I didn't believe in myself.

To my selfless mother for redefining the
meaning of love and compassion.

Acknowledgment

Firstly, I would like to thank my mother, Dorothy King, for being such a fountain of knowledge regarding this whole endeavor. Thanks also to the late Alice Marler for her original genealogical research and to Ralph Marler for providing additional facts pertaining to the Marler family. As well, it should be noted that some creative license has been taken by the author concerning minor details in Part One. Finally, all names (except for public figures) have been changed to protect personal identities in Part Two.

Contents

Introduction

It is obvious that our family history helps define who we are genetically. But what about the emotional aspects involved in our personal makeup? Beyond the fascinating study of genealogy, I wrote *Seasons Out of Time* in an effort to better understand the background leading to my birth.

However, this meant that in addition to revealing events to be proud of, I also had to confront the "skeletons in the closet" that accompanied the same journey. This is reminiscent of when President Abraham Lincoln was having his official portrait painted. The artist asked him if he would prefer to have his many facial imperfections brushed out of the final creation. "Paint me, warts and all," came Lincoln's ready reply. Who am I to disagree with such a distinguished figure?

In researching this book, I reached back through 165 years in the telling of this story. This led me to tackle such controversial topics as the possibility of predestination and the perplexing meaning of life. On that note, I welcome you to fasten your seatbelt and join me on this remarkable odyssey.

PART ONE

The Ancestors

Somewhere in Missouri
(1861—1865)

The river ran red with blood. It was as if God had taken a giant can of paint and indiscriminately brushed the exposed clay banks with broad streaks of crimson. Bodies lay motionless in heaps all around, while still others floated strangely serene-like downstream. The sound of human moaning, crying out in pain and desperately seeking attention, could be heard in the distance. Walking briskly, the sickening stench alternated between the smells of burnt gunpowder and rotting flesh. This was no place for a lady.

Mildredge "Millie" Bilyeu wasn't supposed to be there. The drinking well her family had been using had recently become contaminated and could no longer be relied upon. They couldn't wait any longer, she surmised. With her husband out collecting firewood, Millie had left their children with a family friend and was taking a shortcut through the forest in a desperate attempt to retrieve water. But as she got closer to the river's edge, the formerly thick screen of trees that a person could have counted on for protective cover in the past, became increasingly sparse. Fierce cannon fire had reduced this part of the once full-grown forest to nothing more than a series of stubs, broken and limbless, not unlike many of the soldiers spread out on the blood-soaked ground before her.

Millie was weary, but astute, knowing that even though this particular battle might be over, the Civil War raged on. Awestruck at the surrounding devastation, it was hard to tell who had won here, if anyone. The Union Army, in which the state of Missouri was a member, outnumbered the Confederacy considerably in both manpower and weapons. This pragmatic woman couldn't help but wonder, if this was the scene on her side of the river, imagine the carnage in enemy territory beyond.

The Civil War was a major turning point in the history of the United States. The four years of fighting between the states often pitted relatives against each other in many families. With differing priorities, the industrial North was interested in maintaining the Union, while the agricultural South was intent on preserving a way of life that had become dependent upon the practice of slavery.

President Lincoln, referring to the 18 free states and 15 slave states in 1860, described the nation as "A house divided... half slave and half free." Considering such conditions, a national conflict like the Civil War was inevitable.

With the introduction of new methods of fighting and advances in weaponry at that time, the magnitude of such a war being fought on home soil was unheard of. One recent study has revised estimates of the number of casualties, now suggesting that upwards of 750,000 men had been killed or wounded, costing more American lives than all other wars combined since then.

Unable to comprehend the scale of human tragedy that had recently unfolded any longer, Millie's mind drifted back to memories of a simpler time...

Miller County, Missouri (1849)

Mildredge "Millie" Bilyeu had met her future husband, Daniel Brumley Jr., in grade school. Being born and raised together in the same local county, it was the kind of place where everyone knew each other. Their respective families had been good friends for many years and encouraged the two emerging teenagers to date one another. In keeping with the standards of that era, Daniel and Millie wasted little time and were married in 1849. He was a fresh-faced 16-year-old, while she was still the tender young age of only 13.

Abiding by the expectations of a frontier society still experiencing a rugged lifestyle, the young couple would go on to produce nine children over the coming years. Their children's names included some unique monikers, almost characteristic of those you might find populating a riverboat steaming up the mighty Mississippi at the time: Winnie California, John Madison, Caledonia, Thomas J., Minnesota, Benestra, Sarah E., Arizona Artie, and Clemen Deanally.

Caldwell County, North Carolina (1850–1859)

The warm autumn weather of 1850 ensured the many farmers of the "Tar Heel State" with a good harvest. The fertile farmland produced an abundance of crops: tobacco, corn and cotton, in that order. Plantations were large in North Carolina. And being a Southern state, farm labor was cheap, coming in the form of slavery.

Having been appointed administrator of his father's estate two years earlier, James Benton Marler was one of those farmers. With a sprawling plantation to manage, he had been raised to assume the role of prosperous farmer and landowner.

James proudly surveyed the bumper crop of neat rows of bright-leaf tobacco, widely used for smoking, chewing, dipping and snuffing. His land stretched virtually to the horizon. Having taken over all of his father's assets, this included becoming the owner of 16 black slaves, one of the largest slave owners in the county. This ownership provided him with a calm reassurance, practically guaranteeing success in bringing in this year's crop.

There was another reason to celebrate the harvest this year. After having been considered to be quite the "catch" by numerous local women for many years, 20-year-old James was going to settle down and get married on October 29. A relieved Martha Ann Stewart, older than her new beau at 26 years of age and at risk of becoming an "old maid" if she didn't find a suitable husband soon, was the lucky girl to have finally caught his eye. But like all farmers everywhere, forever concerned with changing weather, the all-important harvest would have to come first.

Once married, time progressed and life proved to be successful for the young couple, with the birth of four children coming in succession over the next nine years. Three daughters: Sarah Elizabeth, Juletta Ann and Alice Columbia would join one son, Samuel Alfred, in rounding out the active household. Life was indeed good and only getting better for the Marler family. They thanked God daily for their bountiful blessings and looked forward to a promising future together. After all, what could possibly go wrong?

Caldwell County, North Carolina (1861–1869)

The artillery shelling of Fort Sumter by Southern troops in Charleston, South Carolina's harbor on April 12, 1861, sealed the fate of an already tense nation. The fuse to the smoldering powder keg that was national politics of the day had literally been ignited. This provocation, happening next door in neighboring North Carolina, caused the states to systematically line up like proverbial dominoes, depending on which side of the legendary Mason and Dixon line they were located on. The Civil War had begun.

The prospect of President Lincoln and his Union forces winning this national struggle would mean the end of slavery. This was viewed as a dangerous threat to the economy of the Confederate states. As far as the South was concerned, nothing should be allowed to jeopardize this long-time way of being.

James Benton Marler knew that the very success of his thriving plantation was closely intertwined with the use of slaves. Like most Southerners in their collective attitude at that time, it was inconceivable for him to think of any other way of life. As long as he could remember, the white man had been in the position of a superior master, with his black counterpart being the subordinate slave. It had always been that way and seemed to be the natural order of things.

At 31 years of age, James would do his duty along with many other able-bodied men in North Carolina, and enlist to fight in the war. He convinced his worried wife Martha that such a battle wouldn't last long, no doubt believing the naive notion himself. Besides, all the other men he knew were going off to fight. It would be a grand and glorious affair for them all to take pride in, something to tell their grandchildren about one day.

North Carolina had been one of the founding 13 states that originally formed the nation. Even though it was part of the South, it tried in vain to preserve the Union, even after most other Southern states had left. But when President Lincoln asked the state to supply troops to fight its fellow Confederate states, North Carolina felt it had no choice but to refuse. The state went on to secede from the Union on May 20, 1861.

More than ten battles were fought on North Carolina soil. It was during one fierce encounter that some Confederate troops retreated, leaving local soldiers to fight on their own. Afterward, the North Carolinians suggested putting tar on the heels of the other troops, so they would "stick better in the next fight." This forever labelled the residents as being from the "Tar Heel State."

As a participant in this national conflict, North Carolina contributed to the Confederacy in a major way, supplying some 125,000 troops. In the end, approximately one quarter of all Confederate soldiers killed came from the state. In retrospect, these odds didn't bode well for any local men who were fighting, no matter what their personal beliefs in glory and courage might have been.

Shockingly, about one-third of the population of North Carolina was enslaved in 1860, the year before the war broke out. For a resident black person of that period, who had probably been born into slavery, they would have known no other existence. No matter how the slave owner might try to justify his ownership and treatment of them, the black person was still living in bondage, the ultimate "property" of another human being.

To help maintain their subservience, it had been illegal to teach slaves how to read or write in the South. So after a lifetime of having been deprived of a decent education and the accompanying life skills that went with it, the average black person would have had some concern as to what would they do and where would they go once free. It would be similar today to an innocent person having spent decades confined to a prison, eager to experience their newfound freedom, only to face the sudden shock of the many challenges of life to be encountered on the outside.

Joining the Caldwell County – E Company / 58th North Carolina Troops of the Confederate Army in June, 1862, James Benton Marler rose quickly up the line of command. Within a year, he was appointed to the rank of 3rd Lieutenant and then climbed to 1st Lieutenant one month later.

E Company was comprised of 174 men, almost all of whom were farmers, and had been fighting in east Tennessee since July, 1862. It was a blessing in disguise that the battlefield was just across the state border, which was a mere 30 miles from

James' North Carolina home. It was there that he would be badly wounded in battle and sent to hospital on June 9, 1864.

Being injured in the war and taken away for medical treatment could be likened to a death sentence, paradoxically, since hospital conditions were notoriously abysmal during the war. Patients faced a drastic lack of medical supplies, with sanitary conditions being almost non-existent. Infection among the wounded was rampant, with disease killing far more soldiers than those who died in actual battle. It was clear that James would never recover in such a place and was fortunate to be sent to his nearby home to recuperate.

By August, 1864, James had returned to fighting and was promptly elected to the position of captain. Attrition in the troops could have speeded up his meteoric rise in military standing, with age also considered as a factor in the decision, but being elected was an honor which meant the most popular person would get the position.

However, James would return home to be with his family in December, 1864. This might have been as a result of lingering injuries from recent combat or due to the birth of his son, James Theodore Marler, on December 15, 1864. At any rate, the family patriarch never returned to the conflict that was still raging not far away.

Fortunately, Captain James Benton Marler wasn't considered to have gone AWOL (away without leave) from the Army. This was because, unlike soldiers of a lower rank, officers were allowed to resign their position.

After almost four years of warfare, it was evident that the Confederacy was losing the war. The "writing was on the wall," as death and destruction abounded throughout the South, which had suffered the worst devastation because most of the fighting had happened there. The traditional way of life in the "land of Dixie," for better or for worse, was on its way out.

Confederate General Robert E. Lee officially surrendered on behalf of the South to Union General Ulysses S. Grant representing the North on April 9, 1865. But it wasn't long before the American people would be thrown into even more disarray. Not even a week later, on April 15, 1865, fate would see President Lincoln give up his life after having been assassinated. The nation would never be the same again.

This new future didn't look very promising for people like white plantation owners, in particular. As a matter of fact, the eventual abolition of slavery would be the impetus for dividing up large plantations into smaller farms. The number of farms in North Carolina alone doubled over a 20-year period from 75,000 in 1860 to 150,000 in 1880.

James and Martha had a big decision to make, one that would not only affect their immediate lives, but of future generations to come. The young couple chose to sell their sizable property for the best price they could get, given the circumstances of the war-ravaged local economy, and made plans to depart from North Carolina.

Having waited until 1869 to finally make the move, James' weak body was loaded onto a covered wagon, along with assorted family possessions. Eldest son Samuel would assist his ailing father, symbolically taking hold of the reins. The rest of the children climbed into a second wagon behind, with Martha assuming control.

It was a bittersweet moment for the heartbroken clan, as they headed down the rural country road, the silhouette of their longtime family home slowly disappearing through a dusty haze behind them.

Heading west, the Marlers would slowly make their way through the rest of the "Tar Heel State," on through Kentucky, bound for Missouri. God had blessed them all to survive the "War Between the States," having guided them to new lives elsewhere. The state of Missouri, often considered a western gateway to the expanding nation, would become their final destination... or so they thought.

McDonald County, Missouri (1878)

Elsewhere in Missouri, John Madison Brumley was 23 years old when he married Sarah Lucinda Williams, a mature 17-year-old, on January 14, 1878. Not long into this new marriage, John developed a recurring stomach condition, woefully misdiagnosed at the time, but getting more painful in its progression.

In those days, with medical doctors being severely limited in what they could do for more serious ailments, desperate patients were quick to try a variety of homemade remedies and word-of-mouth recommendations that might be circulating. Drinking cure-all tonics or sampling traditional Indian medicines was an accepted thing to do.

One of the more popular notions making the rounds at the time was to take in the healing benefits of ingesting the mineral water and soaking in mineral baths of hot springs, wherever they might be found. The medicinal effects were guaranteed to help, according to local elders, who had lived long enough to prove they had been doing something right along the way.

With mixed emotions, newlyweds John and Sarah would bid farewell to their respective families in Missouri, in search of better health prospects for him. The young couple's hope resided in a place called Mineral Wells, Texas. It was there that they planned to relocate and establish their new life together.

Mineral Wells, Palo Pinto County, Texas (1879)

I t is ironic that the last battle of the Civil War took place at Palmito Hill, Texas, near the entrance to the Rio Grande. This historic event transpired on May 13, 1865, over one full month after the actual war had ended on April 9. It had taken that long for the news of the Confederate defeat to reach the soldiers who were still fighting there.

Over the next two decades, settlers and their families, along with investors and their money, would all flock to Texas. Ambitious cattle drives highlighted the 1870s, leading to the expansion of railroads throughout the state in the 1880s. Brave pioneers were eager to tame this new frontier and develop this resource-rich land.

Whether it was the dry Texas air, genuine quality of the mineral drinking water, or simply the "placebo effect" at work, John's medical condition seemed to improve, at least for a while.

Furthermore, his health seemed good enough to start a family, one of the primary goals of any young married couple of that era.

In fact, the Brumleys would produce six children in all: Minnie Isabelle (Belle), Cora Ellen, Effie, Callie, Calvin, and Delila. But there was something special about the birth of their first-born child, Minnie Belle. Her life would go on to reach beyond borders, affecting a multitude of future lives to come.

Collin County, Texas
(1879–1884)

Minnie Belle Brumley was born on February 11, 1879 in Collin County, Texas. Growing up, Belle was petite in size, unique among her four much taller, yet younger sisters. But she more than made up for any such perceived physical "short-comings" with her strong-willed nature and resourceful spirit.

Belle would spend her formative years in the county, north of nearby Dallas. Living there would allow her father the opportunity to make frequent visits to Mineral Wells, located just west of neighboring Fort Worth, and continue drinking in its nourishing water.

Life in Texas, another Southern state still recovering with a post-Civil War economy, ensured tough times for most of its residents. But for a father who was limited in what he could do for work and restricted to where he could live, purely due to health reasons, the Brumley family experienced true hardship.

John and Sarah would join other impoverished white people, along with their black counterparts, picking cotton in the adjacent fields to help support their growing family.

Cotton could only be picked between the morning hours of 6 a.m. until noon, to avoid the unbearable Texas heat that would envelope the surrounding countryside come afternoon. Belle had no choice but to grow up quickly in this harsh environment, serving as full-time babysitter of her junior siblings, while her parents toiled away.

A system known as "sharecropping" gained popularity in the South during the Reconstruction period, which occurred after the Civil War had ended. This was where plantation land-owners, who had vast cotton crops in need of harvesting, would employ freed black slaves and poor white farmers, who could then all share in the profits. It would supposedly be a win-win situation for everyone involved.

The "sharecroppers" would travel from farm to farm, picking fields of cotton, an absolute necessity in making a decent living back then. It was on one of those early journeys that Belle's life took a dramatic turn, bringing about new meaning and proving a personal resiliency that would come in handy for her later on.

The Brumley's covered wagon had been loaded down with a heavy iron stove and other assorted necessary items inside. Belle was around five years old at the time and eagerly joined her parents up front, sitting in between her mother and father.

John took hold of the reins and the horses began to pick up speed. With a combination of the sleep-inducing heat and the horses galloping rhythm, Belle soon became drowsy, slowly drifting off. Somewhere along the route, the wagon went over a bump in the dust-covered road, forcing Belle's slight frame to be quickly ejected from her seat and landing firmly on the ground below. The large wooden wheel rolled over her tiny body, pressing down hard on her delicate chest. Out of breath from the crushing weight, Belle felt light-headed and was about to black out, feeling as if her spirit had left her physical body behind and was now floating effortlessly above.

It was probably a blessing that she had been blissfully asleep and unaware of what was about to happen to her, with her limp body not being rigid or full of fear at that moment. Such an incident happening to someone else of her small size may very well have resulted in the person's sudden death. It was becoming apparent that God had spared Belle's life, wanting her to remain alive in order to fulfill some greater purpose, one that was yet to be revealed.

Palmer, Ellis County, Texas (1885–1888)

It could have been Belle's recent encounter with her near death experience or possibly John's ongoing struggle with his own personal health issues. Maybe it was a sense of futility arising from the vagabond lifestyle of picking cotton or all of these factors combined. Either way, John felt there had to be more meaning to life than mere subsistence. He began to experience an emotional tugging of the heartstrings that accompanies the uncontrollable desire to serve God.

This young man's "higher calling" wasn't something to be taken lightly, but it wasn't a complicated matter to be debated for very long, either. With time being of the essence, it also didn't require many years of specialized schooling.

In those days, the only tools John needed to pursue this new mission were his well-worn Bible, trusty horse and a genuine Christian passion burning from within. The good Lord could be counted on to take care of the rest.

Becoming a Southern Baptist preacher, riding horseback from town to town in a circuit, John traded one set of hardships for another. He was now totally dependent on the generosity of poor rural townsfolk, most of whom had little themselves. Grateful parishioners would provide whatever assistance they could; whether it be in the form of a home-cooked meal, temporary shelter while visiting their town, feed for his hungry horse, or a few spare coins as an offering.

All things considered, John Madison Brumley was following his heart, accomplishing something bigger than himself and for the greater good. If adversity was to be viewed as a bridge to a stronger relationship with Jesus, then John's personal sacrifices as a "man of the cloth" would be well worth the effort. What more could his Creator ask of him?

Mineral Wells, Palo Pinto County, Texas (1889)

It was 1889 and John's health had worsened in recent years. He was making the journey to Mineral Wells more frequently, drinking the water and taking the mineral baths, all in a futile attempt to feel better. He worried about what would happen to his family if he became bed ridden. But now coughing up blood and doubled over in pain on a daily basis, unable to eat solid food and keep it down, the implications were far greater than he had ever imagined.

With John battling what was most likely an advanced stage of stomach cancer, the day came when Sarah gathered the children around to say their last goodbyes to their ailing father. The younger ones didn't quite know what was happening, but Belle fully grasped the gravity of the situation. She knew things wouldn't be easy for the already struggling and soon to be fatherless family, wisely bracing herself for what was to come next.

John died on August 27 at the young age of 32 years. Belle was all of ten years of age herself, being instantly transformed from eldest offspring to assistant breadwinner, virtually overnight. There would be no time allowed to complete the normal transition of a child growing into young adulthood for her.

Now a widow with six children to support, Sarah did what she could to get by, earning extra money through washing other people's laundry. Belle took up the cause by joining the assorted workers in the cotton fields every day, picking the soft white fibrous crop in the relatively cool morning air, then going on to provide domestic help to a wealthy local family during the oppressively hot afternoon.

Working for a family with three children, whose ill mother was recovering from what was known then as "consumption" or tuberculosis today, Belle continued her now familiar role of cooking, cleaning and caring for small infants. Her innate resourcefulness was a must, with her carrying one child on her hip, while preparing meals at the same time. Being short in stature, Belle would routinely have to stand on a step stool to complete her household tasks, including baking bread and changing diapers.

Life had become a matter of survival for the Brumleys since John's death. No matter how hard mother and daughter tried, it was increasingly difficult for them to eke out a living and make ends meet. Throughout this ordeal, Sarah had been in sporadic contact with her family back in Missouri. Being without a husband, with no sign of things about to change in the foreseeable future, she saw no alternative but to accept their invitation to return home.

The Brumley children had all been born in the "Lone Star State." If being Texan meant one was of sturdy stock, resolute and determined, Belle exemplified her birthright. She would view moving to another state as a possible adventure and ticket to a better life. Belle couldn't have been more prophetic in her outlook.

McDonald County, Missouri (1869—1904)

Meanwhile, after having moved his entire family to Missouri and leaving the chaos of the Civil War in his beloved North Carolina behind, James Benton Marler chose to settle in the town of Pineville in 1869. He pursued the only form of livelihood he knew, renting some available land and returning to the life of a farmer. Unfortunately, his war injuries had also followed him along and finally caught up to him. Within five years of arriving in Missouri, James would pass away on July 13, 1874, at the age of 44, in the town of Anderson. His wife Martha Ann and their children were devastated.

James' eldest son Samuel Alfred, being only 17 years of age, would come through for the family once more by assuming the role of man of the house. Being understandably busy in his new position, Samuel would wait another five years before taking a wife of his own, Isabelle Camel Ratcliffe, on November 16, 1879. They would prove to be an industrious couple, in more ways than one, by parenting no less than 11 children during their marriage.

Their children's names represented a time gone by: William Walter, Minnie Gertrude, Bessie Lee, Annie May, Lallie (Lila), Lola, Fannie Myrtle, Thomas Alfred, George Finley, Ollie Belle, and Roy Cecil. And once again, the first-born child would choose to venture down the road less traveled.

William Walter was born on September 30, 1880 in Anderson. It wasn't long after his birth, having outgrown the farm they had been renting just outside of town, that Samuel decided to move the family to what was known as the "Cherokee Nation." More specifically, it was a section of land along the border, referred to as the "Cherokee Strip," having been a Cherokee Indian Reservation in earlier times. Relocating to rented farmland there; the Marler family were now officially living at Cayuga, Seneca Nation, Indian Territory.

This entire region consisted of an existing Indian population that had been growing steadily through the forced relocation of other tribes there, due to long-standing federal government policy. Indian Territory, situated on the doorstep of Missouri, would eventually go on to become the new state of Oklahoma.

This rugged landscape would also become the Marler's new home. Their farm included the usual livestock such as horses, cattle, sheep, and mules. Ambitious as he was, Samuel would also run a sawmill during the farming downtime of the winter months. Located on the fringe of this new territory, being rapidly opened up thanks to bold pioneers, business was good for the sawmill owner.

Growing up, Walter had worked the land in earnest, having a passion for farming like his ancestors who preceded him. But he had also demonstrated having a mind for business, becoming restless as a result, and was eager to pursue more lofty aspirations. By 1902, he was back in Missouri, attending college in Southwest City. Within a year of graduating on the honor roll, he quickly applied his business skills to that of leasing a store selling groceries and other provisions, soon expanding to include a flour and feed operation, as well.

The turn of the century also found the Brumley family, having left Texas a decade earlier, settled into Missouri life. All of the children had been split up early on, being raised by neighbors and friends. Belle was fortunate enough to move in with a loving family, headed by a respectable man named Price, who treated her as one of his own children. She would never forget his kindness to her.

Belle had been working as a live-in servant in a Southwest City household since she had turned 21, during the milestone year of 1900. She had also transformed into a beautiful young lady during that time.

It wasn't long into 1903 when Belle, pondering the future of a career being spent in servitude, approached the bustling W. Marler & Co. general store to purchase household supplies for her employer. As is often the case when two people meet for the first time, when someone least suspects what's going to happen next, that destiny tends to cross paths with fate.

Belle had never seen this store before and was curious as to what it had to offer. Walking inside, she began to browse the well-stocked aisles, repeatedly glancing at a paper checklist in hand. Walter quickly noticed her petite female figure, standing out among the hulking masculine frames of his regular customers, like a beacon shining in a dust storm. Who was this attractive woman and where did she come from, he wondered?

Walter approached Belle, introduced himself and asked if he could help her. It was common practice for a storekeeper to review a customer's shopping list and personally retrieve the corresponding items for them. Anything unavailable could then be special ordered in time for their next visit. Most importantly, though, these two young persons had met.

As was the custom of that era, a man acting in the role of suitor didn't wait long to invite a potential mate out for the purpose of courtship. The female object of his affection usually didn't wait long to respond in turn. With both members sharing the common goal of wanting to raise a family, and the more children the better, time was precious.

Most men would never dream of becoming an old bachelor on purpose, with their female counterparts living in constant fear of the dreaded "old maid" syndrome. This was in addition to the reality of people having a shorter lifespan at the turn of the century, considering the relative harshness of living conditions back then (39 years for the average American in 1900, as compared to 79 years today). All things considered, William Walter and Minnie Belle would soon become a couple.

In the meantime, Samuel was proud of his son Walter's success with a flourishing retail business. He welcomed Belle as a promising new wife for his son, having quickly recognized her maturity and hard-working nature. But Samuel had also grown restless. He was tired of renting someone else's land and dreamed of owning property of his own. Having missed out on the American land rush that had transpired before his time, Samuel realized that such local farming opportunities were a thing of the past in the legendary "Wild West" of the United States.

There must be someplace left where a man could still stake out a sizable section of land, large enough to grow his own crops, reaping all of the benefits and rewards that came with private ownership. But where could he find such a place?

It was during a conversation Samuel was having one day with some of his fellow farmers, the "good old boys" who frequented the W. Marler & Co. general store, when one of them held up a local newspaper. There in big bold letters, an advertisement practically screamed out: "Western Canada – the new Eldorado." Enticing images depicting a lush wheat field having been recently harvested, a happy looking farmer on a horse-drawn hay wagon and a well-kept farmhouse on a picturesque homestead leaped off the page. A further detailed description of the many advantages of relocating to this undeveloped territory reassuringly included: "Homes for Everybody, Easy to Reach, Nothing to Fear, Protected by the Government." If that wasn't enough to pique the curiosity and whet the appetite of any discouraged American farmers, the poster continued: "Wheat Land, Rich Virgin Soil, Land for Mixed Farming, Land for Cattle Raising." The call to action at the bottom of the page exclaimed: "This is Your Opportunity. Why not Embrace it?" But the "piece de resistance" of the entire marketing campaign followed below: "Western Canada Farm Lands – FREE 160 Acres."

The Government of Canada was opening up the western sector of that vast country to development through legislation known as the Dominion Lands Policy. The land was apparently fertile and unbroken, ready for settlement, but just lacking the necessary settlers. The Canadian government was encouraging those who were interested and capable, by offering a free homestead comprising of one 160-acre quarter section of land. For a token $10 payment, the prospective homesteader had to legally agree to turn the sod, effectively breaking the land, planting crops and building a home, all within three years of arrival. If they happened to survive and were successful in this endeavor, land ownership would be their reward.

These ads had gone out throughout Europe and the United States. Enthusiastic settlers, many of whom probably didn't even know where Canada was located on a world map prior, were responding to the promotion in droves. To ambitious souls like Samuel Marler, this must have looked like "manna from heaven," almost divine in its origin and timing.

Later in 1903, Samuel decided to make an excursion up to Western Canada to see for himself if this offer was for real. By now, available land was being snapped up fast, in progression as one headed further west. Traveling first by horseback and then by train, he ended up in the Clover Bar district. This was located across the North Saskatchewan River and east of the fast-growing city of Edmonton, in what was then the all-encompassing region of the Northwest Territories (long since divided up to include the province of Alberta). Samuel liked what he saw and immediately rented some land. He couldn't wait to report the good news upon his return to Missouri.

Arriving back home, Samuel proceeded to extoll the virtues of the wide-open Canadian Prairies; how it was a place where an individual could still aspire to farming rich agricultural land, while being a landowner.

However, this would truly become a family affair. In an almost unprecedented action, all the members of the immediate Marler family would be uprooted and make the move to Canada. No one would be left behind in this venture. This included Walter, who even though he was doing well in his current retail operation stateside, found himself drawn by the prospect of combining his penchant for business with his love of farming. He promised to send for Belle, with their romantic relationship still blossoming, once he got established in this new land.

So it was early in 1904, after Walter had sold his general store for a tidy profit, that him and his father headed to the railway station on their transcontinental mission. To the local townsfolk, they must have resembled the Biblical characters of Noah and his son boarding the historic ark, as they approached the waiting freight car with their eclectic entourage in tow. This motley collection of critters and equipment consisted of: six horses, six cows, four mules, four fox hounds, two wagons, two disc plows, a disc, seeder and harrows, the disassembled sawmill and some assorted household effects. Walter and a male friend boarded the railway car as human escorts on this journey, with Samuel bidding them farewell. The family patriarch would follow with everyone else, later on.

By March 1904, Samuel had made arrangements with the railway company to reserve an "Immigration Car" for the final trip. Loading the remaining family members and their belongings inside, they set travel for Canada.

Belle remained back in Missouri, continuing on with her life as a domestic servant, helping to raise someone else's children in someone else's home. But she had so many questions and concerns. Would she ever be able to pursue a life of being a wife and a mother to a family of her own? Belle knew that Walter was ambitious and driven, following in the footsteps of his father Samuel. And it was evident that he was successful in his business dealings, as well. But what would life be like in this land up north called Canada? For that matter, would she ever hear from Walter again, now that he was living in another country?

Belle began to wonder if maybe this had all been just some sort of fantastical dream on her part, perhaps an exercise in nothing more than wishful thinking. And then the long-awaited letter from Walter appeared. It had taken a few weeks to arrive, but that was to be expected, in a place not that long removed from the time of the legendary *Pony Express* mail delivery.

Apparently, the Marler family had been busy settling into their new home, literally putting down roots in the unbroken Western Canadian soil, having recently brought in their first harvest. Life sounded full of hope and promise, with the local people being helpful and friendly, and the vast prairie sky being the only limit. The one thing missing from this vivid northern landscape, according to a love-smitten Walter, was his sweet Southern Belle.

Rereading the hand-written letter again and again, Belle smiled with a sense of relief and anticipation. Walter had made it sound like their own little private patch of heaven on earth awaited her. But he also made it plainly clear that the choice would be hers, as to whether she wanted to live there or not. She could always return to America if she so decided. He just wanted her to come up for a visit, as soon as she could possibly get away, to see things for herself. With an offer like that, Belle thought, how could she refuse?

Strathcona, Northwest Territories, Canada (1904–1909)

In hindsight, Belle probably couldn't have picked a worse time of year to visit that particular area of Western Canada than in late December. Having been born and raised in Texas, she had no conception of just how cold a Canadian winter could be. And Walter, fully realizing such a potential shock to a Southerner, was prepared for it.

Belle's expedition consisted of her taking a slow-moving train through the state of Minnesota, heading north across the Canadian border to the bustling crossroads city of Winnipeg. It was there that Belle would transfer to another train, this one heading west, scheduled to arrive at her final destination on December 24.

It was of no surprise to any longtime resident that a winter snowstorm was unfolding on the open prairie. This unplanned interruption would delay Belle's anticipated arrival until after midnight on Christmas Day, 1904.

Finally pulling into the Edmonton railway station, Belle was exhausted. Getting ready to vacate the train, she wearily gathered her belongings together. Would Walter even be there to meet her at such an ungodly hour, she wondered? With steam puffing from the tired locomotive and smoke rising from the adjacent building, it was hard to see anything clearly.

Even though the train ride had been a chilly one for most of the way, the biting cold air outside hit her with a blast of crispness, piercing her exposed flesh with a numbness she had never felt before. The temperature hovered near 40 below, with a wind-chill that was even colder. But Belle was also being bombarded with self-doubts and second thoughts. What was this frigid place and how could anyone possibly live here? More to the point, was it too late for her to get back on the train for a return trip home?

Suddenly stepping forward through the shrouded mist of a sparkling ice fog, there appeared an anxious-looking Walter. He was calling out to Belle, eagerly trying to get her attention, while waving a handful of papers.

The couple quickly embraced with a hug and a kiss. Walter grabbed Belle's luggage and headed for the relative warmth of the train station, with Belle following him hurriedly inside. People moved briskly in that kind of bone-chilling conditions, she soon learned. Sitting down on a nearby bench, fully aware of the festive moment, they exchanged mutual greetings of Merry Christmas. Before Belle could finish commenting on the shocking winter climate, Walter revealed the documents he was clutching in his hand. It was an official marriage license. This would turn out to be a special occasion in more ways than one.

The nervous groom-to-be wasn't taking any chances; they would be getting married immediately. As Belle would quickly realize, she wouldn't be returning to the United States any time soon.

Boldly waking a local minister and his wife out of bed at two o'clock in the morning, the marriage ceremony was hastily performed, with the legal documents witnessed and signed. Surreal as this unfolding situation was, Mr. and Mrs. Walter Marler would now set off on a horse-drawn wagon, heading out to their new homestead in the Clover Bar district located east of town. Welcome to Canada!

The geographical boundaries of Western Canada continued to evolve in the early years of the 20th century. There was a reason why one would disembark the train at this point on the wide-open prairies. With the broad North Saskatchewan River approaching dead ahead, winding serpentine-like through the expansive Edmonton river valley and no bridge to cross over it, it was truly the end of the line. As if by providence, however, some of the most fertile soil for farming in the country could be found in this zone.

Strathcona was the municipality located on the south side of the river, established first because of its convenient access to the railroad. But Edmonton was a young upstart, coincidentally receiving city status in 1904 and sprouting rapidly on the north side of the same river.

They were like twin cities, Strathcona and Edmonton, growing and competing alongside one another. When the young government of the newly minted province of Alberta, freshly carved out of the vast Northwest Territories in 1905, was searching for a suitable location for its new capital, the more modern Edmonton was chosen to host the Legislature. Not to be outdone, Strathcona would be provided with another provincial plum, becoming home to the University of Alberta.

The faster growing and larger city of Edmonton would eventually go on to amalgamate Strathcona, absorbing it into its sprawling collection of communities in 1912.

In 1913, the railway and its accompanying "Iron Horse" would arrive in Edmonton with the opening of an engineering marvel of that era, the iconic High Level Bridge. Local development was now guaranteed to move "full steam ahead" from the older south side to the newer north side of the North Saskatchewan River.

Today, an authentic railway caboose adorns the distinctive "End of Steel" park, marking the spot in the quaintly popular "Old Strathcona" neighborhood near where the train had ended its original journey so long ago.

The union of Walter and Belle would signal a new beginning in a new land, along with a new family. With their American roots soon to be firmly transplanted into Canadian soil, the couple would be responsible for conceiving seven children over the coming years. This included their eldest child and only daughter, Madaline Isabel, along with six sons: Samuel Madison, Walter Price, John Kenneth, Lloyd Brumley, followed by fraternal twins Donald Thomas and Douglas Calvin.

If Belle had thought life in the South, post-Civil War had been a struggle, she was in for something else altogether on the untamed prairie of Western Canada. Pioneer life in this part of the world brought with it a unique set of hardships she couldn't have possibly imagined. Taking a log ferry across the river before the water became totally frozen over, arriving at her new home in the isolated wilderness, was just the beginning. Living in a small log cabin, stuffing old rags in between the gaping cracks of rough-hewn logs in a desperate attempt to stem the cold air, became part of one's survival.

Walter had arrived in Canada along with his entire family: three brothers and five sisters, both parents and a grandmother. However, Belle had left all her family and friends behind in the United States, a true pioneer in every sense of the word. Thankfully, the Marlers took Belle in and accepted her as one of their own. This was not only indicative of the close-knit family's nature, but also a sign of the times. In order to not just survive, but actually succeed in the rural west, one had to be accepting of newcomers. A homesteader's nearest neighbors, for instance, most likely lived quite a distance away in this sparsely-populated area. You had no choice but to befriend them, as not only your success, but your very survival could depend upon their future help and assistance.

An eyewitness description of what kind of lifestyle the Marlers had left behind in the United States and what awaited them in Canada, was made by Samuel's youngest son and Walter's brother, Roy Cecil:

> "We arrived at the Immigration Hall in Strathcona on March 12, 1904. Measles were prevalent at that time and I succumbed and made the journey to Clover Bar in a covered sleigh with coal oil lanterns surrounding me, as well as hot rocks.

There were about 100 acres of cultivated land on the farm, with the rest being pasture, bush and the Old Man Creek running through.

My father was an ardent sportsman. He loved fishing, particularly fishing in a boat at night with his baby son, stoking a cedar fire in the middle of the boat. The light from the fire seemed to attract the fish to come near so he could spear them. He always had fox hounds; in the States he hunted possums, squirrels, wild turkeys and raccoons.

When we came to Clover Bar, bush rabbits were as thick as mosquitoes are now. They had well-padded paths up and down the hills of the creek. Coyotes were very plentiful. I counted 17 in one group near where the city lagoon is now. We used to take as many as 125 pelts during the winter months. They sold from $5.00 to $30.00 for really large pelts.

My oldest brother Walter killed a black bear on the south side of the North Saskatchewan River, upriver from the Old Man Creek. We also got a number of Lynx and some deer.

Our fox hounds would trail animals by scent all day and away into the night, returning home late the following day if you could not get to them and kill the wild animal.

My father knew the famous desperado brothers Jesse and Frank James. *(Author's note: The Jesse*

James gang was active from 1866 to 1876, but had previously joined pro-Confederate guerillas known as 'bushwhackers,' operating in Missouri and Kansas during the Civil War.) It was the custom in the Southern States during the end of the 18th century, for almost all of the adult men to carry a gun for protection purposes. Father carried his in a holster under his vest - a 38 calibre Smith and Weston revolver. He would take it off at night and put it under his pillow. After six months in Canada, he put the revolver in the dresser drawer and left it there.

The most unpleasant things I can recall on the farm was the two-storey log house. All the downstairs were in one room and the upstairs had two bedrooms, with a log lean-to used for the kitchen. The one room was used as a living room quarters with two beds in it, a large heating stove, a cloak room and sometimes a dining room. My grandmother smoked a clay pipe and always had a gallon pail half full of ashes sitting near the stove for Uncle Theodore, who chewed tobacco, to use. We boys also liked to put our wet socks and moccasins there to dry overnight. My uncle used to practice squirting tobacco juice through his two front teeth to hit this so-called spittoon. As a result of the condition of my shoes and socks after a night's exposure, it was better to not aim at the spittoon at all, rather than aim at it and miss.

The most lasting memory I retain of the old log house was the bedbugs it contained. If anyone asked about the bedbugs, our reply was that there was not a single bedbug in the house, they were all married and had large families. They were so bad really that we had to leave and sleep in the granary in the summer. There was no D.D.T. in those days and with the cracks in the logs, they had a great advantage.

It had been particularly exciting at times, to have lived on and near the banks of the North Saskatchewan River. The river had been considered over the years as a treacherous stream; a dangerous place to swim in. The cold water, swift and swirling currents, has taken many a life over the past years. Since some time prior to the turn of the century, until about 1920, it had been used extensively for both commercial and passenger navigation. Father often walked to town and built a small raft and floated down river to home.

Steam boats used to ply the river with freight for settlers many miles downriver from Edmonton. They didn't make much noise going downstream, but you could hear them for one or two miles pounding their slow pace upstream. The most exciting time for all concerned was undoubtedly the river flood of 1915. In July, the river flooded its banks and covered many of the so-called river flats above and below Edmonton. At that time, there were only two bridges across the river. The Low Level and the High Level, except the railway bridge at Clover Bar built in 1909. The water came up to four feet of the bridge floor. With debris, small buildings, lumber piles being lifted from their base and floating down against the bridge, concern was great that the bridge may give way. So flat railway cars were loaded with gravel and backed across the bridge to hold it secure. I remember standing on the bank and watching as piles of stacked lumber, hen houses with chickens still in them, small barns, shacks and various other articles came floating by. These of course, came from the river flats upstream from the Low Level Bridge, as there was no clearance for them to get under the bridge."

Roy Cecil Marler (1972)

Belle quickly embraced her new life with a bold determination. Rising every morning at 4:30 a.m., she would begin her day by milking cows, feeding chickens and baking bread. Much of this was done before the male family members had even woken up. The remaining necessary duties of farming, hunting and general building maintenance would be tackled by the men soon enough.

The other female responsibility of bearing children began for Walter and Belle with the birth of their daughter, Madaline Isabel, almost one year later on November 30, 1905. This grand personal event would be matched on a larger scale by the official formation of the province of Alberta during the same year.

The first of six sons, Samuel Madison, would be born one and a half years later, on May 12, 1907. But it was with the arrival of their next son, Walter Price, on February 22, 1909, that Belle would experience her first real tragedy, one that she would never fully recover from.

At the time, Price was born with what was described as having a "hole in his heart." Such a medical condition today could be successfully operated on, prolonging one's life. In the early 1900s, however, there was only one prognosis for someone facing such a health ailment. Little Price's days were severely numbered, with him becoming all the more special as a result.

Meanwhile, Madaline was beginning to show a natural talent for teaching. Burying her head in books, with a voracious appetite for learning, she left the many mundane chores of housework for her mother to do. Madaline soon decided to practice her newfound vocational interest in becoming a teacher with little Price. Using the large family Bible as reading material, a staple found in most pioneer homes of the day, she taught the fair-skinned, blonde-haired boy to read by the time he was five years old. Little Price, being a bright and inquisitive audience of one, responded in kind.

London, England (1914)

At the turn of the century, Britannia ruled the waves, with the British Empire being at its peak as the greatest in world history. As its capital, London was not only the seat of power and influence, but also the largest city in the world. The crowded streets bustled with trade and commerce. You could find it all in London, along with the stark division of classes that so often appears in such a society, from the refined to the impoverished.

British life, full of its many extremes at that time, could be compared to having booked passage on board the RMS *Titanic*. The stately ocean liner, which had been launched with great pomp from the port of Southampton in 1912, would sink unceremoniously a few days into its maiden voyage. Britain was also headed for a major turning point, of which there would be no turning back.

The King family consisted of parents James Joshua and Edith Lucy, along with their four sons, all residing in the district of Wimbledon. The father was an established London book-keeper by trade, with eldest son, 18-year-old Lionel Kenneth, following in his occupational footsteps. The second son, Hubert

George, was 16 years old and still undecided about his future career ambitions.

It was as if Edith Lucy, an already overprotective mother, had been blessed with the gift of prophecy in prompting her to take her next action. Knowing full well that farmers were exempt from military duty, with the practice of farming considered to be an essential service, the decision was made. This very proper English family would apply to emigrate to the former colony of Canada.

Almost without warning, the First World War, commonly known as the "Great War" at that time, descended upon the European continent on August 4, 1914. Many nations were connected through a series of unfortunate alliances, such as Britain, and therefore obligated to defend each other. This wartime commitment extended throughout the British Empire, including such far-off places as Canada.

Having departed the shores of the island kingdom earlier that same year, the Kings prepared to trade in their pencils and accounting ledgers for ploughs and pitchforks, pursuing an agricultural lifestyle instead by becoming farmers on the Canadian Prairies.

Ironically, the same passenger ship the King family had previously sailed on to Canada, the RMS *Empress of Ireland*, sank not long afterward on May 29, 1914. It had collided with another ship in dense fog on the St. Lawrence River in Quebec, killing 1,014 of the 1,479 people on board. This disaster would make it the deadliest maritime accident in Canadian history during peacetime. If not for fate, such a tragic happening as this could have drastically altered the course of events in the lives of not only the Kings, but of others yet to come.

Once in the "New World," James Joshua took his family and headed west to a farm down the road from the small town of Camrose, Alberta. Farming was a tough way of life for anyone, but especially did not come easy for this former pencil-pushing Englishman and his sons. Even though they had relocated to the middle of a colonial backwater, in the eyes of sophisticated matriarch Edith Lucy, at least her family was safely away from the battleground that Europe was fast becoming.

Camrose, Alberta, Canada
(1912–1945)

L ife had continued for the Marler family, along with the births of two more sons: John Kenneth on July 10, 1912 and Lloyd Brumley on August 18, 1916. But there was no doubt that little Price, with his delicate features, loving nature and fragile health, was special.

This only made the fateful day of April 25, 1917, when little Price's leaking heart began to bleed uncontrollably, all the more tragic. Holding him close, the pallid eight-year-old boy died in his grief-stricken mother's arms. An integral part of Belle's world, that which had helped her tolerate the many accompanying hardships of a pioneer woman's life, came to an end that day. This resolute woman, who had already come so far and endured so much, would never truly be the same again.

The first year after little Price's death would prove to be the most unbearable for Belle. She would go through the motions, completing her daily chores, but then head over to the nearby riverbank overlooking the fast-flowing North Saskatchewan. To some in her position, such a discrete vantage point as this could have been interpreted as an opportunity to end her inconsolable heartache. Instead, it was there where no one else could hear her, that Belle could cry out in painful anguish. Even though she had known from the beginning that her frail little boy's lifespan would be unpredictable and drastically shortened, it made no difference in the end.

It became obvious to Walter that his distraught wife was seriously hurting. And it really didn't come as much surprise when Belle told her husband that the memories were just too difficult to deal with anymore on their Clover Bar homestead. With Belle's sanity at stake, and knowing that he couldn't succeed without her fully functioning by his side, Walter agreed to her request to move. He would go on to purchase a three-quarter section of land in the small farming community of Camrose, some 60 miles away, on August 21, 1917. Maybe there, they could attempt a new beginning, once more.

Leaving their first Canadian home and all of Walter's close relatives behind, the couple relocated their growing family to Camrose the following year, in 1918. Setting up their new farm on the southern outskirts of town, time carried on for the Marlers.

The "Great War" had been raging in Europe for four years. Even though the young nation of Canada was heavily embroiled in this conflict, eventually losing over 60,000 soldiers, it had left the rural-dwelling Marler family relatively untouched. This was because they were busy working farmers, a task and occupation considered to be an absolute necessity during wartime. The risk of vital food supplies becoming scarce during a period of increased rationing was ever-present. But more specifically, no one in their young family was of fighting age. However, this would change as the "war to end all wars" would fail to live up to such a lofty goal in the years to come.

In the meantime, there was something else transpiring of urgent concern; a catastrophic by-product of the war's widespread destruction and its resulting unhealthy living conditions. The deadly Spanish Flu epidemic of 1918-19 was spreading quickly, having entered Canada through returning troops, leaving no corner of the country untouched. It would go on to kill 21 million people worldwide, including approximately 50,000 Canadians, often attacking the young and healthy unexpectedly. This included pregnant women, the same condition that Belle found herself to be in, once more.

The armistice ending the First World War took place at the momentous time of 11 a.m., on the 11th day of the 11th month—November 11, 1918. Later that evening, at five minutes to midnight, the first of fraternal twin boys, Donald Thomas, came into the world. Five minutes after midnight, the second twin, Douglas Calvin, arrived. Because of the unique timing of their births, the day of November 12, 1918 was officially entered onto their birth certificates.

Giving birth was a risky experience at the best of times, but especially due to the Spanish Flu being at its peak. The newborn babies could have perished early on if not for Belle being relatively isolated on a farm and able to nurse them to health. They would be the last children she would ever conceive.

The following decade, characterized by the good times known as the "Roaring Twenties," would be succeeded by another extreme period – the "Great Depression." And the

Marler family would expand yet again, but in a different way. Within ten years of Belle giving birth to her twin sons, she would go on to become a grandmother herself.

With both Madaline Isabel Marler and Hubert George King living on separate farms in the surrounding area, visiting the nearby town of Camrose regularly to purchase supplies, such a meeting of the two would have been reminiscent of how Walter and Belle had first come together when they were young.

The ensuing marriage of the Marler's first-born and only daughter, Madaline, to "Bert" King on March 8, 1927, would happen in due course. And Walter and Belle would become grandparents one year later on April 16, 1928, when Hubert Marler King was born. Two years after that, on April 7, 1930, Dorothy Madaline King would accompany her older brother. Another generation had now joined the expanding Marler clan in Canada.

The era that Hubert and Dorothy were born into was a turbulent one, to say the least. It was as if the fates had mysteriously come together, conspiring to deal multiple blows to an unsuspecting society. This happened with a succession of tragic world events. First came the stock market crash of 1929 and its resulting economic collapse. Next was the unprecedented drought conditions known throughout North America simply as the "Dustbowl."

Canada was amongst the worst affected countries of the world by the Depression, because one third of its Gross National Income came from exports. And the rural-based economies of the four western provinces, being heavily dependent upon exports, were hardest hit.

If the extended Marler family had not been living on a farm during the miserable Depression years, along with their livestock and large garden, they could have starved. The same would have been true for other farming families in the area, including the Kings not that far away.

Unfortunately, all was not marital bliss for Madaline and Bert King. Living under the same roof with her pretentious mother-in-law, Edith Lucy, proved to be a daily challenge for an independent-minded "free spirit" like Madaline. Bert's strict English mother strongly adhered to the old-fashioned colonial belief that North Americans were somehow of lower class, inferior to their former British masters.

Therefore, in addition to her new role of farm wife, Madaline was expected to hastily fall into line and submit to being the obedient servant of proud Edith Lucy. New husband Bert knew his place in the domestic pecking order and didn't dare stand up to his overbearing mother.

The "writing was on the wall" for the young couple. Having been raised on a prairie farm, Madaline always felt out of place. Milking cows at the crack of dawn had never been the life for her. And becoming the wife of a recently transplanted English farmer later on must have seemed familiar, yet foreboding. After six long years together on the farm, Madaline and Bert separated. Considering the King family's very British roots, they never actually got a divorce, as the authoritarian Church of England would have frowned upon such a prohibited activity.

Tired of feeling like a square peg in a round hole, Madaline decided to pursue her original dream of becoming a school-teacher. She would go on to teach in the one-room schoolhouses of her day, ever-present throughout the provinces of Alberta and Saskatchewan. This included teaching her youngest brothers, Douglas and Donald, in the first grade.

Taking her students and her job very seriously, she would dutifully stay after school and help any slow learners to keep them from failing. Parents bemoaned her as their children would arrive home late for their chores. It was no matter, as she was determined that any pupils entrusted to her would pass.

But what would become of her own two children, Hubert and Dorothy? Who would raise them and where would they reside? It was initially proposed that if Madaline didn't want to become the maid-servant to Edith Lucy, then daughter Dorothy could take her place. Having previously bristled at the thought of such personal oppression, Madaline had vacated the family picture by then, with no one left now to defend her children's best interests. Hubert had the advantage of being an older boy and was therefore able to escape the conflict created by these living arrangements. Dorothy would be given no choice but to drop out of school, expected to spend her time being trained to serve her demanding English grandmother.

It was 1936 and the King family was coming to a crossroads. The father, James Joshua, had been ill for some time. He had become almost reclusive, due to increasingly poor health, rarely emerging from his bedroom. The inevitable death of patriarch James Joshua happened unsurprisingly, later that same year.

Along with the newfound challenge of the traditional male head of the household now missing from the scene, the King family dynamics were quickly altered. Matters only got more complicated with the ongoing absence of Madaline. And so it was that Edith Lucy, who had been gradually assuming more and more control over family affairs during her husband's protracted illness, took charge completely. She had no time or patience to debate the welfare of her granddaughter, firmly believing that she was right, as usual. As far as Edith Lucy was concerned, Dorothy was a child and a child's place was to be seen and not heard.

When Belle got wind of what was happening at the King family farm, she decided it was time for a visit. Remembering her own former life as a household servant, Belle confronted a stern Edith Lucy, who was now surrounded by her watchful sons.

"Dorothy is not your slave!" declared Belle, firmly voicing her strong disapproval of their plans for her young granddaughter. "She deserves a better life than that!"

"We are of superior British heritage," countered Edith Lucy, "while you Marlers are of nothing more than lowly American stock. It's obvious that we know what's best."

"That's what you think!" replied a defiant Belle.

"You can't talk to my mother like that!" yelled one of the King sons, rushing forward in the heat of the moment.

Belle was undaunted. "Then tell her not to say foolish things!"

The crux of the matter was that impoverished living conditions, due to the "Great Depression," were at its worst. If Dorothy couldn't serve as Edith Lucy's domestic help, then she couldn't remain living there. And if her single father was too busy trying to eke out a living as a farmer, something that didn't come natural to him in the first place, then poor Dorothy was left in a state of limbo.

Out of desperation, the dreaded notion of adoption was proposed as a possible solution. After all, life was hard and times were tough. Could anyone really afford one more mouth to feed, let alone have the time or energy required to raise another child?

In preparing Dorothy for adoption, it was arranged for her to board a train that would take her to Edmonton in order to conclude this sad affair. It seemed as though her fate was sealed. This entire undertaking must have appeared to be like "déjà vu" to Belle, looking back on what she had gone through as a young girl after her father had passed away.

The verdict was in; Belle had made her decision. The Marlers would take in both Dorothy and Hubert and raise these two grandchildren as if they were their own children. There would be no further argument from the Kings on this matter.

The winds of war, never having truly been extinguished after the last worldwide military confrontation, were blowing across Europe yet again. With the invasion of an unprepared Poland by an aggressive Germany in 1939, along with the previous pledge of a still war-weary Britain to defend the Polish people in such an event, the Second World War had begun. The sparsely-populated nation of Canada, being an active member of the British Commonwealth, was committed to yet another international conflict.

As was the custom, if you were a farmer, you didn't need to go to war. Your services were required at home to supply food for the country. In the Marler clan, the most suitably aged candidates for fighting were their two youngest sons, Douglas and Donald. Being that both boys were fraternal and not identical twins, their respective health conditions were very different. Due to his poor eyesight and wearing glasses, Douglas was allowed to enlist in the Army and went on to complete his basic training there.

It was 1940 and Donald was a student attending the Guelph Agricultural College in Ontario. He could have remained there to complete his studies, but having good health and yearning for adventure, was eager to get involved in the war effort.

Against Belle's better wishes, Donald enlisted to fight in the Royal Canadian Air Force. He would learn how to fly at one of Canada's many Commonwealth Air Training schools, where young men would arrive from a variety of nations to acquire their so-called "wings." Donald trained at the school located in Guelph and was so adept at flying, that he was offered the opportunity to remain there as a flight instructor of future pilots.

Donald had no desire to watch his fellow airmen fly off to Europe and leave him behind. Being born and raised on a prairie farm, Donald viewed this as a golden opportunity to not only participate in a noble and worthy cause, but to experience the excitement of seeing the world at the same time. The newly-minted Flight Sergeant couldn't wait to go overseas.

The local newspaper proudly chronicled the young soldier's wartime adventure with the following story headlined:

SGT. MARLER SEES
GERMANY FROM BOMBER

"Sgt. Donald Marler, who landed in the Old Country (Britain) on New Year's Day 1942, tells his parents Mr. & Mrs. Walter Marler in a letter written September 7, that he went on his 'first excursion' on the night of September 5 to Germany and "I must say they have some very beautiful lights. Every color of the rainbow. They gave us a warm welcome and we were welcome to everything they had, but being on the British side I refused their hospitality and came back without a scratch. We put on a good show and left many fires. The smoke rose to about 8,000 feet... am going on another trip tonight, so wish me luck. These raids are not nearly as dangerous as I had anticipated. In fact, I'm not worried at all (much)."

The Edmonton Journal

It was obvious from Donald's dispatch that he was trying to use humor in an attempt to downplay the ever-present danger of these bombing missions, if only for the sake of calming his already worried parents. But from the sarcastic tone present in the enthused pilot's letter, concerning the kind of enemy reception him and his fellow bombers were receiving over Germany, it would soon become evident that this air campaign was not going to be a quick one-sided affair.

As a matter of fact, the Royal Canadian Air Force would prove integral to the management of the British Commonwealth Air Training Plan. And with numerous Canadians serving in Britain's Royal Air Force, Bomber Command's job of night bombing Germany was a dangerous task. The eventual death of nearly 10,000 Canadians in this command was proof of that.

Back on the home front, Belle insisted that Walter make sure that at least one of her sons enlisted to do battle would be brought home safely. Walter obliged by simply requesting that Douglas be discharged from the military, as he was required for farm work. Ironically, the military training complex was in an area located at the north end of the Marler farm, which later became the Camrose fairgrounds. It kind of gave new meaning to the phrase "home on the range."

With winter being around the corner in early November, 1942, hunting season had arrived in Canada. This was a very significant time of year, if you lived in a rural area of the country. A person could hunt a wide variety of wild game, including such animals as deer, elk, and moose. This was not done for sport alone, but rather to complement a family's valuable food supply during the harsh weather conditions of the coming months. The carcass of the dead animal would be taken to the local butcher, where the all-important meat would be prepared and packaged, to be used as a source of protein. The remaining trophy head would hang proudly on one's wall afterward, as a triumphant reminder of the event.

It was in anticipation of this annual ritual, a rite of passage if you were a young man living on a farm, that the Marler sons set off on their hunting expedition. They didn't have to venture too far away, since there was bush and forest all around. One could expect a light dusting of snow to be found on the ground by now, with the change in seasons typically happening much earlier and being more extreme out West.

Walking through the dense woods, the eldest son Sam led the way. He was more experienced on these missions and knew where to go for the best hunting grounds. Youngest son Doug would follow behind, bringing up the rear on this outing.

It could have been a protruding tree root, or maybe a submerged gopher hole covered by snow. There were certainly plenty of both these kinds of obstacles to be encountered along the way. No matter, Doug had stumbled over something as they walked, causing his shotgun with the hair trigger to go off. The sudden jolt threw him backwards. In an instant, Sam let out a cry and fell to the ground. He had been shot in the leg and was bleeding profusely.

The boys scrambled to Sam's aid, fashioning a tourniquet to stem the flow of blood. They knew it was imperative to get him back to town for medical attention, as urgently as possible. They also knew that this tragedy had been an innocent accident that could have happened to anyone, given the circumstances. The old shotgun was defective and should have been disposed of long ago. There would be no blame circulated among the family concerning this mishap and rightfully so.

The Camrose hospital was small, understaffed and lacking in medical supplies. This was not unusual at the time, since the ongoing war effort had drained funding and redirected much-needed resources such as doctors and materials. This rural medical facility, which had always served its purpose in supporting the local community in the past, would soon be put to the test.

Sam was rushed to the hospital at once. Ironically, the attending physician was an old friend of Sam's from his high school days, the two of them having been fellow students together. The first priority was to attend to the 35-year-old man's massive loss of blood with immediate life-saving transfusions. Hopefully, this would help stabilize his condition.

Sam's unsuspecting parents, Walter and Belle, were hastily summoned. They were informed that there had been a terrible hunting accident, but their first-born son was in good hands at the nearby hospital. Surely, he would recover from this dreadful incident.

Within days, Sam's health deteriorated, with him contracting a fever from a fast-spreading bacterial infection. Sam had developed gangrene from the wound to his leg. The young doctor knew he had no choice in this matter. If his good friend was to be saved from certain death, the injured leg would have to be amputated. The doctor would have preferred that Sam be transported to the big city of Edmonton, 60 miles away, where more extensive medical services awaited. Unfortunately, there was no time for such a journey.

Dealing with both a lack of pain-killing morphine and the proper anesthetic required for such surgery, the doctor proceeded to amputate the leg. You could hear Sam screaming, semi-conscious and writhing in pain, from far down the hospital corridor.

These efforts would all be in vain, however, as Sam succumbed to his injury and passed away on November 4, 1942. He left behind a wife, Ruth, and two children, daughter Joyce and son Ronald. This was in addition to his grieving parents, siblings and numerous friends.

Upon reflection, Walter and Belle's first two sons, Sam and Price, were both deceased now. It has been said that a parent should never have to bury their child. It's also been said that deaths come in threes.

Belle was still in an obvious state of mourning, when the unthinkable happened. With a knock at her front door, she received the fateful telegram, less than a week later on November 10, 1942. Her son Donald, fighting in Europe, had been listed as Missing in Action and presumed killed the day before on November 9, 1942. Once again, the local newspaper had an update:

> "SGT. Pilot Donald Marler, 24, son of Mr. & Mrs. Walter Marler of Camrose, listed missing in action overseas, in November and presumed killed. Born in Camrose, he went through high school there and afterwards attended Olds Agricultural School, Provincial School of Technology in Calgary and one term at Guelph, Ontario agricultural college. He enlisted with the Royal Canadian Air Force in May 1941, received his wings in the following December and went overseas at first of last year, serving latterly as pilot of a Halifax bomber. Wing Commander of his squadron wrote to the family that he was one of the most promising men in the squadron."

> *The Edmonton Journal*

Within less than one week, Belle had lost two sons, on two different continents. The fact that Sam had perished from a hunting accident virtually in her own backyard, while five days later Donald would be shot down a world away by the Germans while fighting over North Holland, made no difference. She loved them both dearly as their bereaved mother.

To say that a person dealing with such unimaginable loss and its accompanying raw emotions would be feeling numb at that point, would be a gross understatement. The fact that Belle was resilient and able to get through this personal anguish was a testament to her strong character, past experience and most importantly, her faith.

Coincidentally, it would be 20 years later in 1962 when Belle and Donald's fraternal twin brother Douglas would visit his final resting place. Having completed 47 bombing missions over Europe and North Africa, Donald had been buried along with his entire crew side by side in the Commonwealth War Graves on Texel Island, North Holland.

Belle had received the distinct honor of being named a Silver Cross mother by the Canadian government. Now mother and son were invited by the Dutch government to travel to Holland. While there, one of Belle's fondest memories was having tea with Queen Wilhelmina of the Netherlands.

Belle couldn't help but reflect on the hard and difficult times that she had experienced throughout her life, both in the United States and in Canada. Maybe if she had never met Walter in the first place, following him to Canada to start a family there, she would have been spared all of this tremendous grief and heartache. But she also realized that if her marital union with Walter had never transpired, she would have never known the fantastic love and joy of the family that she helped conceive and raise.

Life for Belle wouldn't be easy in the aftermath of these events and she would have to approach living by taking things one day at a time. Such a human spirit as she possessed, a true wonder in itself, would thankfully prevail. She reminded herself that she had two more children to care for now, her grandchildren Hubert and Dorothy, both of whom would require her time and attention. In hindsight, having such renewed parental responsibilities would prove to be her saving grace.

Walter had always been public-minded while living in Camrose, having served for many years as a town councillor and also Reeve of the municipality. This extended to him also serving on numerous agricultural boards and being one of the original signatories of the Alberta Wheat Pool, the non-profit organization tasked with selling the province's important grain.

Three years later, in June 1945, Walter would finally retire from farming. Belle, who had been experiencing physical health problems for a while, required kidney surgery. Upon closer examination, her kidneys were packed with multiple stones. It was suggested that this had come from her drinking well water on the farm, which was known for being notoriously high in iron content, for many years.

One of Belle's kidneys could be saved, but the other was beyond salvation and needed to be removed. What better reason could there be to finally move to Edmonton, as such medical surgery and its subsequent follow-up care had to be done in the much larger hospital there.

As a matter of fact, the predisposition for developing kidney stones would go on to affect numerous Marler children and their offspring down the road. For example, Douglas would subsequently be required to have one of his kidneys surgically removed, too.

Hubert and Dorothy would follow Walter and Belle, relocating to a small house in the older Norwood neighborhood of Edmonton. In addition to the practicality of making such a move, maybe the change of scenery and pace of life would help Belle deal with all her memories, as well.

Somewhere in Poland
(1949)

The Second World War had been over for about four years. Much of Europe was in ruins, with countless refugees displaced and on the move. Poland, where the military conflict had officially begun, had been one of the hardest hit nations and would take years to recover.

The Pekrul family had come through this turmoil and survived almost intact, save for the father, John. But it had been one long battle of endurance for mother Martha and her two sons, Eugene and Adolph, during the war years and soon after.

Riding a train headed for a coastal port, full of other war-weary exiles in search of a better life elsewhere, the Pekruls had plans to board a ship bound for Canada. There had been a variety of vessels transporting wave after wave of similar immigrants, en route to the Canadian port city of Halifax, Nova Scotia. The Pekruls had been fortunate enough to secure passage on one of them. And because they already had relatives living in Canada, residing on farms outside of Edmonton, Alberta, that would become their final destination.

As the train hurtled down the tracks, passing countryside they would never view again, the family reminisced both openly and silently. It had not been an easy time for any of them.

Being of German descent, but living just across the ever-changing national border in Poland, the Pekruls owned a small farm complete with an apple orchard. The father, John, was strict and ruled with an iron fist. The eldest son, Eugene, was mild-mannered and compliant, taking after his mother. However, the youngest son, Adolph, had always been a loner and a rebel. Adolph emulated his father with a characteristically hot temper, making him virtually unapproachable by others, often getting into fights with anyone who dared to cross him.

Having a strong work ethic, the Pekruls made a life for themselves as best they could on their farm. That was until war was declared with their adopted country being invaded by the fatherland. It wasn't long before Nazi troops marched across the transparent border, rounding up all the local men in the town square. As Adolph watched from a distance, his father and uncle were lined up and issued an ultimatum by the German commander in charge. Either they would join the Nazis in battle, essentially fighting against their new neighbors, or they would be executed on the spot by a firing squad.

Neither John, nor his brother Rudolph, could bear the thought of taking up arms and doing such an unspeakable thing. Without giving such a horrendous proposal a second thought, both men were summarily shot and killed.

Adolph was horrified at what he had just seen and knew immediately what he must do. Ignoring the obvious birth order, with Eugene being the older sibling, Adolph decided that he would take over as head of the family now.

Time passed and the war raged on, with the occupying Nazis eventually finding their way to the Pekrul family farm. The mother and her two pre-teenaged sons were confronted and taken away, only to be loaded onto a freight train with other local residents. They were told that due to hard economic times, they would all be relocated to somewhere better, purely for their own good, of course. Martha and Eugene naively believed their captor's story. Looking around the cramped cattle cars full of panicked people, Adolph instinctively suspected the worst.

Thinking this would probably be a one-way journey for its frantic passengers, Adolph started planning his family's escape. Once the large wooden door was slammed shut behind them, the train slowly pulled away from the station. The car heaved back and forth, with slivers of light shining through the surrounding gaps of the vibrating door.

Adolph found his way to one of those cracks around the doorframe and glimpsed outside. The train was moving fast down the tracks now, passing dense forests along the way. Grabbing the inside of the door with his strong hands, he was surprised to be able to slowly slide it open. Turning back to the astonished crowd, he called out to his mother and brother. This was their only chance, he told them, to gain freedom and avoid possible death. They had no choice but to jump.

To Adolph's dismay, his family was scared and hesitant. After all, jumping from a moving train was dangerous and what would happen if they got caught? Guiding Martha and Eugene over to the partially opened door to show them how easy it would be, Adolph surmised the time for talking was over. Pushing his brother out the door first, he then grabbed his mother's hand and jumped, pulling her with him.

The trio rolled down an embankment, landing bruised but uninjured at the bottom, as the train rolled onward. They would go on to live out the remainder of the war by picking berries in the woods and foraging for scraps of food from sympathetic farmers in the area. Their continued existence would be a daunting series of challenges, with Adolph having bravely saved his remaining family members from an outcome of certain death.

Edmonton, Alberta, Canada (1950–1956)

Surprisingly, Walter and Belle had adapted well to the confines of urban life in their small wartime home in Edmonton. Their grandson, Hubert King, had lived with them for about four years, worked up north for one year and then gotten married in 1950 to his new bride Eileen. The newlyweds had since moved on and were getting ready to start a family of their own. However, granddaughter Dorothy King was still single, working as a secretary for the post-war wage of 90 cents an hour, and residing at the Marler home.

Belle was concerned for her granddaughter's future. What if something should happen to the elderly couple, Belle worried, leaving Dorothy on her own and unable to support herself? Dorothy's father, Bert King, was also a retired farmer, now living on his own in the town of Camrose. Meanwhile, Dorothy's mother, Madaline, had been busy pursuing her passion as a schoolteacher in small towns and rural communities throughout the West. Neither parent, constantly struggling to make ends meet themselves, was in a position to support their daughter.

So it was with a combination of relief and trepidation, when the young immigrant named Adolph Pekrul was introduced to Dorothy by a girlfriend in June 1955. For some reason, her girlfriend didn't want to date him and was eager to pass him along, thinking he might be "right" for Dorothy instead.

Adolph was virtually "fresh off the boat," spoke broken English and now going by the westernized name of Ed. In meeting Dorothy, he saw someone who was attractive and well-educated, English speaking and Canadian-born. Ed couldn't wait to introduce her to all his German relatives living in and around Edmonton.

The big day came on August 18, 1956, with Dorothy King walking down the aisle to wed Ed Pekrul. It was stormy weather outside, rain-soaked and deprived of sunshine. Perhaps this was merely foreshadowing of things to come.

Edmonton, Alberta, Canada (1973)

It had been a long time in coming, almost incomprehensible to anyone who knew of Walter and Belle's strong independence, but the elderly couple could no longer look after themselves in their own house. A nursing home was found first for Walter to move into. But with limited facilities available in those days, Belle would have to be put on a waiting list.

Dorothy didn't think twice about offering to take Belle into her home. She was only too willing to reciprocate in the loving gesture previously shown to her by her grandparents, earlier when she was in transition. And everyone knew that Granny would be well taken care of by Dorothy, who had always been seen as more of a daughter figure in the family, anyway.

After three months of this mutually agreeable living arrangement, a bed in the same nursing home as Walter was found for Belle. But she wouldn't reside there for long, as on May 2, 1973, Minnie Isabelle Brumley, long-time wife of William Walter Marler, passed away peacefully at the accomplished age of 94 years old.

For months after her death, Walter could still be found wandering down the hallway to visit Belle's old room, in search of his lifelong companion. Later that same year, on December 26, 1973, one day after what would have been their 69th wedding anniversary and while battling severe pneumonia, Walter struggled with his final breaths and joined Belle in also passing away. He was 93 years old.

It was truly the end of an era. At the time of their deaths, Walter and Belle had 12 grandchildren and 21 great grandchildren. Their legacy in both the Clover Bar district and later the town of Camrose in Alberta, had blazed the trail and paved the way for generations to come.

On the Marler's original Clover Bar homestead, being located in a province rich in natural resources, it was no surprise when something valuable was found buried beneath the land. The couple had unknowingly sold their farm before many tons of gravel would be revealed on their former property, so didn't benefit financially from the lucrative discovery. But a large working quarry continues to operate there many decades later, mining the valuable rock once concealed by the bountiful crops planted above.

The quaint city of Camrose, bisected by the calm reflections of white swans swimming on picturesque Mirror Lake, has grown into a vibrant community of over 17,000 people today. Being strategically located along a vital crossroads of highways and railways; Camrose is virtually guaranteed a "rosey" future. What better tribute to these two maverick pioneers, Walter and Belle, than to have a major residential street named "Marler Drive" running through what was once their cherished farmstead.

From Southern Belle to North Star

Truth is stranger than fiction. Growing up, I would often hear many of the aforementioned stories, awestruck with the fascinating characters and events involved. And because of my mother Dorothy's strong personal attachment to Walter and Belle, their modest house soon became our family's second home.

Looking back, I am left to wonder how different things would have been for so many people, if Belle had decided to remain in the United States in the first place, or had been subsequently scared off upon her winter arrival in a frozen land called Canada. Entire generations of family members would never have existed, including myself. In the grand scheme of things, it all came down to the personal courage and staying power of this one extraordinary woman.

Maybe it was the context of the times when Belle came into being. The year 1879 was witness to a number of worldwide achievements: Thomas Edison demonstrated electric light, perfected the filament light bulb, and then produced incandescent light at Menlo Park, New Jersey. The first electric railway opened at the Berlin Trades Exposition. Sir Sandford Fleming proposed Standard Time, through dividing up the world into 24 set time zones. Madison Square Garden opened in New York City, displaying North America's first artificial ice skating rink. The first automated telephone switching system and first cash register were both patented. Albert Einstein (physicist), Will Rogers (American humorist), Leon Trotsky (Russian revolutionary), Joseph Stalin (Russian dictator), and E.M. Forster (English writer) were all born. Pioneering times, indeed.

Lies My Father Told Me

It wasn't until almost 20 years after my father, Ed Pekrul, had died in 1988 that the whole truth would be known regarding his past life. After speaking with his surviving brother, Eugene, about their mutual upbringing, our family was stunned at what we learned.

We were informed that our father's version of wartime events had been a matter of revisionist family history. Eugene hastened to add that he had always assumed we knew the truth, being equally shocked that what we were now being told was such a revelation to us.

As it turned out, my father's explanation of tragic circumstances concerning his father and uncle being rounded up and shot by the invading Nazis, due to their noble refusal to join enemy ranks, had all been fabricated. This included Ed's heroic efforts to save his vulnerable family from being threatened by the menacing "jackboots."

In fact, the German cross-border invasion of their Polish town did happen. But when the local men of fighting age had been assembled for possible recruitment, John and his brother accepted the offer to enlist with the Nazi army. The two sons and their mother had seen John on one or two occasions after that, when the soldier had been given temporary leave to visit home. The family patriarch had appeared before them, dressed in full Nazi uniform, along with a standard-issue gun on his side.

That would be the last time they would have contact with John. With the war dragging on and Hitler's dream of world conquest waning, they had heard a rumor that he had been shipped along with other troops to the Eastern Front in Russia. Knowing how that desperate battle ended, John was never seen of again.

Likewise, there had been no transport of his family in a train's crowded cattle car headed for a concentration camp, with no daring escape or possible starvation, afterwards. In reality, the mother and her two sons had been sent to separate male and female camps for displaced persons, but only after the war had ended.

The remaining Pekrul family members did indeed join other post-war refugees in heading to Canada, having accepted the freedom offered by the young nation and meeting up with relatives already settled in rural Alberta.

The reasons why my father would have considered spinning such an elaborate yarn and maintaining this work of fiction throughout his adult life would have been numerous. Canada had fought alongside the Allies from the beginning of the Second World War in helping to defeat Germany. And there was a personal connection with my mother's uncle, Donald Marler, having died while valiantly battling the German Luftwaffe over Holland. As well, it would have been far easier for a new immigrant to gain sympathy and pity in his pursuit of a wife and ultimately marriage, especially from a soft-hearted young lady like Dorothy.

New Beginnings

O nce again, I contemplate the prospect of an alternative future if certain events hadn't unfolded as they had. For example, if the Second World War had never transpired, causing its massive movement of war-weary populations, my existence and that of my siblings would never have come to pass. In addition to the many millions of innocent people who lost their lives in this tragically senseless war, there were also countless people born in the following years, as a result of new couplings like my parents.

This begs the question: Is there such a thing as predestination? In other words, are we merely human chess pieces being moved around in this glorious game called life, where the final outcome for us has already been decided in advance? Such an examination of human affairs is reflected in the family migrations of the Marlers escaping the aftermath of the American Civil War, the Kings setting sail from England before the "Great War," and the Pekruls having fled Poland following the Second World War – only to have their respective paths intersect in a remote corner of Western Canada.

Like a cake recipe being mixed in a bowl and then baked in an oven, my resulting DNA was bound together by the complex ingredients of all three clans associated. But a person is obviously much more than the physical, flesh and blood. An individual's psyche is continually being molded and manipulated by the evolving conditions in which they live.

Keeping those profound thoughts in mind, my own personal journey continues...

PART TWO

The Descendants

Dread and Circuses

I t is evident that we don't choose the family that we're born into. If I had known what was in store for mine at the time of my birth, I think I would have just stayed inside and ordered "womb service" instead. There would have been much less emotional baggage to deal with, and I could have handled the running commentary quite easily. But my mother had other plans for me and out I came.

I was an introspective kid growing up, with an insatiable curiosity about things. But I wasn't just daydreaming about what made the grass grow green, the sky shine blue, and the snow fall white. I would wonder how busy singers like Frank Sinatra and Petula Clark must be in the 1960s, traveling from radio station to radio station across the land, repeatedly performing their hit songs live and in person. Think of the logistics involved packing all that equipment, with entire orchestras in tow, just so that he could do it "his way" and she could do it "downtown."

Or what about this man Jesus that I kept hearing about in my youth. He must have been pretty special to have been born on Christmas day, perform all those wondrous miracles, and then die a few months later at Easter. How He was able to accomplish everything that He did in that short time frame and have a best-selling book written about Him was beyond my young mind. No wonder His name kept popping up in conversations wherever I would go.

As a child trying to fit into the role of eldest son in my disintegrating family, life was serious business. I wasn't allowed the natural privilege of a carefree childhood. Growing up quickly was the order of the day in our household. Being placed on the fast track to adulthood, I failed to appreciate the amusing qualities of clowns and couldn't understand their entertainment value to my peers. In my opinion, clowns were scary and frightening beings to be avoided. Circuses bordered on boring, parades were to be endured, magicians were phony, and Halloween was an excuse for organized begging. I was slowly forgetting how to smile or laugh, taking on an aged sense of pessimism before I even knew how to tie my own shoes.

Dreaming is Believing

When I was around eight years old, I started to have a recurring dream over the next few years. It always began and ended in precisely the same manner. And I knew it wasn't a nightmare, because there was never any fear connected. I concluded there was a message to be learned in this ongoing recurrence; I just didn't know what it was until many years later.

This childhood dream of mine would begin with me hearing a knocking at the back door of our home. I would calmly walk through the kitchen on my way to the back porch, place my hand on the doorknob and turn it. Before I could take another breath, the door would swing open, and a mighty rushing wind would pour past me. I would hang on tightly, looking to see who was there. I never saw anyone and couldn't speak, for the wind was so engulfing in its fury. Just when I thought I couldn't hang on any longer, I would wake up.

As an adult this dream finally made sense to me as I sat through a church service one Sunday morning. The pastor was describing how Jesus would knock at the door to our heart and wait for us to answer. If we accepted Jesus into our life, the Holy Spirit would come and fill us to overflowing, being likened to a mighty rushing wind. It all came together for me. God had been trying to tell me that He had a plan for my life, providing both meaning and a purpose that I had long sought after.

Lone Star State of Mind

My father, mother, older sister Dianne, younger brother William, and myself the middle child portrayed the players in our version of a "nuked family." The stage would be set for a continual battle of paternally "old country" ways versus maternally modern thinking, along with birth order role playing that would redefine sibling rivalry.

We all lived together in a modest little house located in the middle of the street in a blue-collar neighborhood in Edmonton, Alberta. The city of Edmonton is known primarily for two things: Wayne Gretzky and *West Edmonton Mall*. It's rather telling when your claim to fame is either a retired hockey player who was traded from the local team and left town almost three decades earlier or the nation's largest shopping center.

The way I see it, the big mall is like dinner theater. Why should I have to be bribed with an all-you-can-eat buffet in order to enjoy live theater? It's as if you couldn't drag my dead body to witness the works of Neil Simon or Tennessee Williams, unless I was allowed to slurp daiquiris and stuff myself with potato salad at the same time.

Likewise, if I'm in need of new socks and underwear, why should I have to be enticed to drive to the world's largest parking lot, ride the world's largest indoor roller coaster, and be submerged by submarine in the world's largest indoor lake, just to get my shopping done? By the time I'm finished experiencing the *Mindbender* and *Deep Sea Adventure*, I've forgotten what business I'd entered the mall for in the first place.

As for the "wild rose" province of Alberta, it is comparable to being the Texas of Canada. With everything from oil wells to office towers, cowboys to cattle ranches, rednecks to roughnecks, and an accompanying deep-rooted aversion to central government – the similarities between these two "mini-republics" are endless.

Alberta is a panorama of contrasting geography and attitudes. Being Albertan comes with having a particular outlook; an undeniable brand on your being that sets you apart wherever you go. It means sharing an old-fashioned belief, naïve as it may seem today, that one person can still make a difference in a cynical world.

Y'all Come Back Now, Ya Hear!

Most of our neighbors were of Eastern European descent, predominantly Ukrainian, and worked in nearby meat packing plants. Our small house was the kind that school children like to draw when describing where they live – literally a square box with a triangular roof on top.

At any given time, you could always smell what was being slaughtered at the meat packers. The steam-powered whistle of the largest plant would blow like clockwork, with birds taking to flight and dogs barking in tandem, signifying the end of another workday.

Living next door to us were our neighbors the Kirbys. This mixed-up clan consisted of Wilbur the hen-pecked father and Stella the obese mother – the perfectly shaped "10" husband and wife couple if you ever saw them standing together, adding their brood of four children to the equation.

Sharing a similar home as ours, the main difference between our properties was the Kirby's appreciation for junk collecting and its indiscriminate distribution. They were among the original "hoarders," with everything from old newspapers to cardboard boxes stacked from floor to ceiling inside. Nothing was ever thrown out or given away there. If something broke down or no longer worked, it would simply get redistributed to their overflowing junkyard outside. If the many scraps of wood items such as broken baseball bats and hockey sticks began to accumulate, Stella would start a backyard fire on their rusted old barbecue, declaring for all to hear that the billowing smoke was a good mosquito-repellant. If we complained to Wilbur that we were tired of smelling like smoked meat, Stella would do her part for "loving thy neighbor" and promptly add more fuel to the fire *(in more ways than one)*.

Stella wore the oversize pants in her family. Her resentment for our household only grew greater as we grew older. Maybe she thought that because the children in our family could learn in school, unlike hers, it was cause for jealousy. Maybe she thought that because our mother had ethics and morals, unlike her, it was cause for anger.

I can only speculate as to what drove this mean-spirited woman to openly spy on us, running from window to window, lurking around corners, and leaning over the fence, watching our every move. But she would go on to become the piranha in the goldfish bowl that was our lives.

There was never a dull moment living beside this bunch of misplaced hillbillies. The mother, having had four children by three different men and being married only once throughout it all, was blatant in her callousness and bold in her manipulation. Stella would continue her affair with another man, the father of two of her children, during much of her marriage with Wilbur.

Assorted residents of our neighborhood would shake their heads in disbelief at the antics of Stella and her boyfriend. He was a pig farmer and would pull his beat up old pickup truck into the Kirby's back alley driveway every morning, just as Wilbur would head off to work from in front of the house. Stella would time it so that her lover would remain there until mere moments before Wilbur would arrive home at the end of his shift. Their timing was always impeccable, until one day...

The morning started out just like any other. The pig farmer pulled his pickup into the driveway, but this time with a full load of pigs on board. It was a case of "the swine leading the swine." With a crude plywood canopy overhead and a metal gate behind, he didn't give his grunting cargo a second thought as he entered the house. Many hours later, his daily visit almost complete and the husband on his way home, pandemonium erupted. Pigs were squealing and running every direction, up and down the alley. Some neighborhood children had decided that rather than frying on someone's breakfast plate, the innocent porkers should be set free.

With the help of some sympathetic, if not bemused neighbors, the pigs were rounded up before Wilbur really "brought home the bacon." Stella always seemed to be daring fate in this manner. Maybe it was just her way of telling humanity that she really didn't care what anyone thought about her.

Lions and Tigers and Neighbors, Oh My!

At some point in your life, you inevitably find yourself in the wrong place at the wrong time. I did one summer day as a young boy. I've never been much of a fighter myself, but happened to witness a match going on between the Kirby's youngest son and another neighborhood kid. Like waving a red flag before an incensed bull, the next thing we saw was Stella, larger-than-life and charging down the street to rescue her son.

The kid who had started the fight in the first place quickly ran through a yard and down the alley to the safety of his home. In the heat of the moment, I too ran for cover. Finding what I thought would be the relative safety of the far side of a neighbor's house; I stood there in hiding, but not for long. Stella rounded the corner, grabbed my slight frame by both shoulders, and began to repeatedly beat my head against the stucco wall. Looking like a wild animal that had just been uncaged, her notoriously hot temper was revealed once again.

A frightened look materialized over Stella's face, as she suddenly realized what she was doing. Just as quickly as she grabbed me, she now released my limp body to fall to the ground. I was left to stumble home crying, only to tell my mother of the latest incident involving the Kirby's. It would be but one of many outlandish episodes to transpire from living next door to that toxic family over the coming years.

People didn't sue each other much in those days, so nothing more came of it apart from the occasional heated exchange between my mother and Stella. It didn't matter to my father what had happened to me. He would usually frequent the nearest bar after supper every night anyways, leaving the true parenting up to his wife.

If my mother dared to approach her husband with any of their children's problems, his uneducated response was to react with violence against the innocent victim. It was of no concern to him that someone else was to blame. Such an attempt at intelligent conversation, considered commonplace in a functional family, was a dangerous exercise in futility in mine.

I would eventually develop excruciating headaches from the beating to my skull; so bad that it affected my appetite for eating. Upon returning home from school every day, all I could do to bear the pain was to lie down on our living room couch, using a pillow to shield my increasingly sensitive eyes from any bright light.

This would continue until an eye examination revealed that the muscle behind my left eye was causing it to turn inward. By the time the necessary surgery was performed, a permanent reminder of a lazy eye lingered behind. My migraine-like headaches, however, were thankfully relegated to history.

A Christmas Peril

The elementary school that I attended was located across a broad grassy field from our home. Sitting at my school desk, I would just have to glance over my shoulder and out the window for a clear view of where I lived.

After yet another night of my father's violent drunkenness, my mind would wander to daydreaming of what a normal family must be like. Watching *The Brady Bunch* on TV, I was convinced that this television family must be indicative of how everyone else lived at the time. All I knew was that our problems certainly weren't solved in a half hour and sure seemed a whole lot worse than poor Marcia's latest pimple outbreak.

Most people have memories of at least one distinguished teacher who made a difference during their childhood. Mine was no exception with a dynamic sixth grade teacher named Mr. Beacham. His innovative teaching methods and encouraging ways helped guide me out of the timid self that I was withdrawing into. He was always coming up with new ideas in which to involve the children of our school with the surrounding community.

One of those ideas that Mr. Beacham had was for our sixth grade class to meet after school one winter's night and go Christmas caroling throughout the area. My enthusiasm for this festive event rapidly dissolved into trepidation as we entered the street that my family lived on. *How embarrassing it would be*, I imagined, *if we all gathered in front of my home for standing room only viewing of the latest knock down, drag out encounter between my parents.*

As the throng of singing children neared my house, someone in the crowd exclaimed they were certain I lived nearby. The teacher asked me if this was true and which house was mine, causing a lump to form in the back of my already warbling throat. Yes, it was, I admitted, assembling everyone to perform for my new family in front of my neighbor's place. Pointing at a stout man and his startled wife staring out at us from their living room window above, I now had surrogate parents. The curious Hungarian couple might not have known what we were all bellowing about outside their house, but undoubtedly would have been proud of their adopted son.

Hunting Season

The day came when my mother gathered us children around the kitchen table to ask our opinions on whether she should divorce our father. It was a Norman Rockwell painting gone wrong, a scenic reversal of how other families might get together to discuss plans for their next vacation. The choice was simple: stay married, risk serious injury and even death, or take a chance on living a decent life. For once we were all of one mind – it was time to move on without this very dangerous man in our daily lives.

After my parents divorced it was like all hell broke loose with neighborhood gang members declaring "open season" on our now fatherless family. My father had never come to our defense when my parents were married anyway, but was a symbolic head to be reckoned with nonetheless. Leading the pack of bone-picking scavengers was none other than Stella Kirby herself.

Being the dominant force that Stella was in our community, she basically let it be known through her youngest son that any mischievous actions taken against our family were fine with her. The gang responded by carrying out the usual juvenile pranks of repeatedly egging our house, having taxicabs and pizza delivery drivers come calling in the middle of the night, and batting baseballs through our living room window.

We called the police, only to be informed by investigating officers that without a father figure present in our family, we were considered to be nothing more than "sitting ducks." Besides, this was typical behavior that many people have come to expect from restless youth. The real torment, however, was yet to come.

Even after all our run-ins with the Kirby's throughout the preceding years, my mother would bristle at the thought of any of them ever hearing our family fight or argue.

"What will the neighbor's think?" was her standard reply.

For her children to ever appear unkempt in public or even consider leaving any clutter in our yard was tantamount to committing a serious crime.

"What will the neighbors think?"

The frustrating irony of it all, after living next door to the original *Sanford and Son* rubbish emporium all this time, drove me beyond distraction.

Moving on to junior high school was full of hope and promise for me; at least until the same bullies that prowled our neighborhood migrated in that direction as well. These gang members were relentless in their cruelty, making sure everyone could see the invisible target they had subconsciously painted on my back. Because there were so many of these punks around, my mother decided to label them the 'goons.'

I couldn't step outside of our yard without being shoved and taunted all the way to school. And I knew it was pointless to even contemplate fighting any of them, since the real cowards always traveled in a pack.

If I saw the gang heading my way in time, I would be reduced to hiding in bushes to avoid any possible confrontation. Was there no escape? What was I becoming?

The mental anguish didn't cease for me once at school. While there, the 'goons' would deliberately parade by whatever classroom I was in at the time. With open doors throughout the antiquated building, anyone could hear them yelling, calling me such degrading names in the process.

Can you imagine actually trying to learn something, other than bitterness and revenge, in that kind of tension-filled atmosphere? Any recent friends of mine would end up avoiding me like I was "*Leper-man*," the new anti-hero, fearful of being tarred with the same sadistic brush. Teachers were powerless to stop this from happening, since they obviously couldn't be where I was at every moment. My life became one of isolation, and I became a loner because of it.

The one area that I stubbornly refused to compromise my values on was the classic youthful desire to conform to the ways of the "in" crowd. I had practically leapfrogged my adolescence in order to become the man of the house after my parents' divorce. This premature maturity of mine prevented me from seeing the value in getting drunk, taking drugs, or vandalizing public property just to belong.

My stubborn willpower, only strengthening the more I was harassed, would serve as a double-edged sword in my battles. Instead of flying under the radar like other non-conforming peers, I made a conscious and deliberate decision to go directly through the line of fire.

On a Chicken Wing and a Prayer

The possibility of my family moving to a better neighborhood and us attending decent schools was simply out of the question. My mother never received one cent of alimony from my father after their divorce settlement. It was a major feat just securing child support payments from the man. Even then we would have to divide up that amount, originally intended for one child, amongst three children instead. Divorce court laws were extremely lax in the 1970s, with "deadbeat dads" being the result.

By now my mother was working as a low-paid sales clerk at a discount department store. With three growing children to feed and sporadic child support coming from my father, she would skillfully stretch our meager budget to afford cheaper food and barely pay our bills with what remained. When preparing our daily meals, she would ration the limited supplies first to her three children, standing back in the cramped kitchen to receive whatever was left over.

Unfortunately, a person's mindset becomes ingrained with such an impoverished way of living after a while. In order to cope with poverty day in and day out, you learn to accept it. If you don't, you feel like you're setting yourself up for nothing but disappointment later on. Just as success breeds success, the opposite can become a self-fulfilling prophecy. It is a paradox that the acceptance of it being your lot in life also helps to guarantee the continuation of this undesirable lifestyle.

Redneck High

When it came time for me to transfer over to high school, the same 'goons' with the same hostilities followed me once more. I didn't know how much longer I could take of this.

I began to empathize with black people and other minorities when I would hear about the racist treatment they had to undergo as the price they paid to walk the earth with their fellow human beings.

Intolerance and conformity was the name of the game being played at "Redneck High." The only difference between here and my old school was that there were now even more and bigger recruits to join the 'goons' in their oppressive pursuit.

Alliances were quickly formed between people who desired the inherent protection that belonging to a gang or being friends with one of its members would provide. I tenaciously maintained that it was my right to attend school, hopefully learning something valuable in the process, and not having to join a mindless herd of sheep in order to do so. There would be a price to pay for such an attitude as mine.

The latest British invasion was also taking place with the birth of the punk rock movement. Arriving with the music, there appeared the blue-haired girl at my school. Administrators could have charged admission as gawking teenagers would crowd around the doorway to whatever classroom the blue-haired girl was in. She could have just stepped off the mother ship, *The Far Side* cartoon-style, complete with sign reading: "Kick Me!" taped to her back.

This was a place where students seeking retribution would casually explode pipe bombs under their rival's car hoods and future felons-in-training would patiently wait for the moment the teacher stepped away, brazenly ripping up textbooks and showering the shredded pages out the windows onto the schoolyard below. The blue-haired girl actually wanted to stand out amid this anarchy, while I dreamt endlessly of blending in.

I soon realized that in order to survive this ordeal, I would have to alter my life as a student and be alert at all times. For instance, I didn't dare enter a school washroom, walk down a hallway, or go near the cafeteria at lunchtime. With teachers "circling the wagons" in the staff room, most public areas were off limits, considered to be a "no man's land" for an unconnected person like myself.

Being tripped with my books flying in the air, pushed down stairwells, or slammed into lockers by the courageous 'goons' who were too fearful to ever undertake their dirty work while alone, became my existence.

Out of a feeling of total desperation and against my better judgment, I decided to pack a jackknife and take it to school one day. I didn't intend on using it for anything other than scaring away any 'goons' in possible future encounters. It was my attempt to even the odds a little after years of persecution, taking back some of the personal rights that had been stolen from me so long ago. Hopefully, I would never find the need to actually produce it.

A few days later, forgetting for a moment that I lived under a state of self-imposed martial law, I made the mistake of venturing down the deserted hallway to my locker during lunch. I was reminded of my folly when I heard the voices of three 'goons' approaching on patrol.

"Let's get him!"

Observing their quickened pace out of the corner of my eye, they reminded me of big game hunters stalking defenseless prey in the wild.

Having no desire to become their latest trophy, I nervously turned my attention back to the top shelf of my locker. With only seconds to go before my anticipated beating, I reached for the knife and extracted its long shiny blade. Holding it tightly in my hand, I whirled around in time to catch their attention before it was too late. They froze in their tracks.

"You wouldn't dare!" remarked one of the trio.

"Just try me!" I responded bluntly.

We silently stared each other down, like animals smelling for any scent of fear coming from their opponent. After seemingly measuring my potential for bluffing, they shrugged and moved on, laughing as they disappeared down some stairs.

I placed the knife in my pocket and took it home after that, never to return it to school again. In retrospect, things could have gone terribly wrong as emotions heated up that day. We were all so fortunate that the outcome hadn't been a deadly one.

This was not a video game we were playing or an animated cartoon we were watching, where the fictional characters could be killed off one moment and rise up the next, living life business as usual.

In a society with a different gun culture, one or more of us would have probably been standing there with a handgun instead of a knife. Long before Columbine had made the news, my high school might have been in the headlines for a similar tragedy.

Like Mother, Like Son

Returning to the relative security of my home after school every day, I would find my understanding mother patiently awaiting my arrival. But living in the "House of Chaos" could be compared to stepping into someone else's nightmare at times.

"Get in here quick," she would often say.

Gently grabbing my arm and pulling me inside, all doors would be systematically shut behind me, supposedly keeping out any neighbor's prying eyes and ears. I would then be informed of the current crisis in progress.

"You'll never guess what's happened now. Your dad is in the Detox Center again and they want you to come and pick him up."

Most of the time I relished these mother-son moments of getting together in our living room. It would give me the opportunity to "spill my guts" to someone concerning the adversity I had to deal with as part of getting an education. For the sake of my sanity, it was imperative that I get things off my chest.

My mother sympathized with my plight, promoting her female brand of pacifism as the answer to dealing with the ignorant 'goons.' As far as she was concerned, it would be best for me to ignore these bullies altogether. This way, I would at least be able to claim the integrity they would never possess.

Then it was my mother's turn, updating me with the continuing saga of the latest bizarre dealings with my father. Just because my parents weren't married to each other any longer didn't mean that my volatile dad had disappeared from the scene. He would regularly make his presence known, if only to continue stirring the already boiling pot.

Mother and son would console each other in the meantime, providing the beneficial moral support that most people seek. She would become my much-needed confidante and best friend along the way.

A person can only take so much stress in their life before they reach a breaking point. Mine finally came when I went for a walk one day, having defiantly skipped a class at school. I headed to a nearby overpass that provided a stunning view of Edmonton's lush river valley, with a busy freeway of traffic directly underneath.

I stood there in a daze, analyzing in my mind what kind of life I had lived and the kind of mental torture I had to look forward to on a daily basis. *Why should I bother trying to endure this any longer? What was I trying to prove anyway? It would be so easy,* I thought, *to simply climb over the railing and jump. My teenaged life and all its heartache would be over in a matter of seconds. I would then be finally free.*

A voice inside me intervened. *Would I really be free?*

During the daily talks I had with my mother, she would often discuss her strong faith in God. I could never quite fathom what had kept her going in the face of all the physical and verbal abuse, alcoholism and poverty that she had to cope with as a result of having married the man she did. Believing in a living God and praying to Him provided her with the strength to continue on.

I was informed that our heavenly Father would be there to shine a light for us at the end of the dark tunnels of life, promising to exchange our personal despair for eternal hope, if only we believed. Unlike my earthly father, full of all the lies and broken promises that an alcoholic comes to represent; God would never let me down.

At the thought of such a supernatural source of power I could rely on forevermore, I was given the assurance that things would get better for me. Snapping out of the trance-like state that I was in, I stepped back from the railing at the edge of the bridge. The non-stop traffic continued far below, with drivers unaware of my presence overhead. Ending my life prematurely was not what God had created me for. I too had the strength to carry on.

Things did improve in my life after that, particularly at school. Having a personal relationship with a righteous God, I was assured that justice would be served, whether in this life or the next. This allowed me to let go of the natural human desire for vengeance and the all-consuming hatred that accompanies it.

With this new outlook allowing me to be more at ease, I was hired for my first part-time job, working as an usher at a live theater complex downtown. It would introduce me to the grown-up realm of employment, along with a taste of culture and some spending money as an added bonus. Most importantly, it would divert my attention away from always feeling like a victim and replace it with a newfound sense of self-confidence. The 'goons' also seemed to sense this new aura of self-respect emanating from within me, choosing to finally leave me alone.

Gall in the Family

I'm terrible at physics, but even I know that for every action, there's an equal and opposite reaction. The so-called "domino effect" produces the same outcome with family dynamics. If someone pushes you, you either fall over or push them back. The chain of life is inextricably linked together, weak links and all.

As adults, we deal with the trials and troubles that come our way in whatever fashion we were familiar with while growing up. But what if your parents didn't teach you any of these much-needed coping skills in the first place? My mother's own parents had separated not long into their marriage, but failed to get an official divorce due to the negative stigma attached to such taboo things during the "Great Depression" years of the 1930s.

I couldn't imagine my grandparents having ever been married to each other. The day it dawned on me there was a reason for their common surname and that they had actually been a couple at one time was truly shocking. They had been separated for so long, with my grandmother even boycotting her own daughter's wedding, all because my grandfather would be giving the bride away. It was considered almost treasonous to ever mention one of their names while in the company of the other. Was there a pattern forming here?

Now under intense pressure to assume the responsibilities of two parents in one, my mother would wrestle daily with the contrary nature of being maternal nurturer, paternal disciplinarian, breadwinner, housekeeper, and defender of the family in hostile environs. She couldn't afford to merely revert back to the inexperience of her own upbringing in reaction to the circumstances thrust upon her. It was a no-win situation for her from the start; one that many people wouldn't think twice about walking away from.

My mother's parenting abilities would be repeatedly put to the test. Following the rules of birth order, William was the last-born child admitted to our three-ring circus. He had witnessed how our first-born sister derived her self-worth from being competitive in life and overachieving at school. Meanwhile, I was striving to find my middle-born niche by learning how to compromise and collaborate, using humor as my attention-getter and survival technique. William was left to blaze a whole new trail in a landscape of decreasing options. He would soon learn that in our splintered family unit, increasingly preoccupied with a "survival of the fittest" mentality, it was to his advantage to not be seen and not be heard.

After surviving his entire childhood as an adult in disguise, William almost died at the age of 16. He had mistakenly chosen to deal with the countless stressors in his life by not dealing with them at all. By keeping his problems and worries to himself, he fell seriously ill.

Near physical collapse, my mother and I literally dragged William to the Emergency ward of the nearest hospital to find out what was wrong. With one look at his ghostly white skin and apparent lack of energy, the medical staff rushed him in for immediate tests. Facing imminent death, blood transfusions were begun. A multitude of tests and eight units of blood later, it was revealed that William was suffering from internal hemorrhaging due to a bleeding ulcer.

With an ulcer that was so far gone in the damage it had done, permanently destroying William's stomach lining as a result, no medication was able to alleviate the pain he was feeling. Unfortunately, eating food and even drinking water would prove to be constant irritants to his raw digestive system.

Daddy Dearest

My father was the one individual who, more than anyone else, was responsible for us putting the "dys" back in "functional." This misguided man can be best described during the first session I had with a therapist. I'll never forget that visit...

I hurried down the hospital corridor. Looking at my watch as I walked faster, the sign at the end of the hallway loomed ever larger. I swallowed hard as my eyes focused on it – 'Psychiatry.'

The door swung open and I walked briskly inside. Glancing around the waiting room, there were people of all ages to be found. In one corner sat a teenaged boy wearing handcuffs, a police officer hovering over him. The boy fidgeted in his seat. I wondered if he was embarrassed at being in handcuffs in such a public place.

"Can I help you?"

A nurse had noticed my 'fish-out-of-water' look. No doubt she had seen it many times before.

I soon found myself sitting in a much smaller room. There was nothing to indicate the nature of work that was conducted here, except for a strategically placed box of tissues on the corner of a desk.

A young man entered and quickly dimmed the lights. We proceeded to introduce ourselves. He certainly didn't fit my image of a stereotypical psychiatrist. With an athlete's build and a 'pretty boy' face, he could have been my age.

"Your family doctor referred you to me. Tell me why you're here today," he inquired.

I didn't know where to begin.

"It's my father," I stammered. "He's dead now. You know, I couldn't shed a tear at his funeral. My brother and sister were crying, though. And now I have such overwhelming feelings of guilt."

Looking up from his rapid note taking, the therapist prodded me.

"Tell me about your father. What kind of a man was he?"

"My father had grown up in a battle-scarred Europe during the Second World War and had a ferocious temper. We 'danced on broken glass' when around him.

I remember waking up in the morning as a little boy to the smell of boiled coffee and the sound of the bubbling percolator. My mother would be neatly packing my father's lunch bucket. I would run to the back door just in time to kiss him goodbye, my lips pressing against the sandpaper-like stubble on his cheek. I wanted so much to have a close relationship with the man. However, I would learn to fear his arrival home at the end of the day," I sighed.

"Why was that?"

"I was a very picky eater as a child and a skinny little boy at that. I would find ways to hide the food I didn't want to eat, like stuffing mashed potatoes under the rim of my plate. Then when you'd pick up the plate, there would be a ring of potatoes left behind on the table. Almost artistic, you know?

Well, my father had no time for this kind of rebellion and would smash his fist down hard on the table. Everything would jump, including me. He would then chase me to my room and inflict my nightly beating. This scenario would become routine for the two of us.

In my simplistic child's mind, I reasoned that only a 'bad boy' would get beaten so frequently by his father. Believing that I must somehow deserve this punishment, it soon became customary for me not to eat everything I was given. That way, when my father inflicted the ritual punishment on me, I could perversely believe that it was justified."

I felt drained, but must have looked like I was going to cry. My therapist motioned at the box of tissues before me. I shook my head from side-to-side. I hadn't cried in years and wasn't going to start now, I'd determined.

As if trying to make me shed those stubborn tears, he pressed further.

"Tell me what was your worst memory of your father?"

That was easy.

"One night, when I was around 10 years old, I awoke to my mother's cries for help. My father had come home drunk and was beating her in the bathroom. Alcohol had become his cure-all. He had beaten her before, but this time seemed different. As

I stood there watching in stunned silence, I honestly thought he was going to kill her.

She saw me out of the corner of her eye and pleaded with me to call the police. I ran to the phone and dialed the operator. But I couldn't tear my eyes away from the scene before me, too afraid that he might finish her off if I did."

I paused, reliving the horrible memory in my mind's eye.

"What happened next?" the therapist asked.

"I had frozen. I couldn't speak into the phone. It was as if I was somehow detached from the moment, like watching a movie. By now my father saw me and knew what I was attempting to do. He grabbed the phone out of my hand and slammed it down. Then he returned to my mother.

She saw that this method of getting help was going to be fruitless. In desperation, she begged me to run down the street and get our neighbor's, an English couple we had become friends with, to call the police instead.

Standing on our neighbor's front porch, shivering in my pajamas on that cold winter night, I rang the doorbell. When the door opened, I burst into tears.

"You've got to stop him. He's going to kill her!"

The police soon arrived, only to find my father stumbling around outside. He was searching through a snowbank, pathetically looking for his precious bottles of beer that my neighbor had wisely taken away from him and hidden there.

I became a light sleeper after that incident, worried that if I dared to fall into a deep slumber at night, my mother might not be alive when I would awaken the next morning. I feared that if something dreadful were to happen to the one responsible parent in my life, what would I be left with? A child can only experience such feelings of insecurity for so long, before they begin to view their environment through a lens of instability.

Arguments had become the standard of communication in our household. So after a trial separation, my parents finally ceased pretending they had a marriage and got a divorce."

My therapist was writing feverishly by now. I was curious what his notes would reveal, if only I could see them.

"How were things after your parents divorced?" he looked up long enough to ask.

"It was strange. I was in the hospital and had had eye surgery the day before they divorced in April 1972. The following day, recovering in bed in my darkened hospital room with a patch over my left eye, I was busy entertaining myself after dinner by bouncing leftover Brussels sprouts into an open closet.

First my mother came in to visit and then left. Next was my father's turn. Without either of them mentioning they had just come from the courthouse, I instinctively knew from their separate visits that it was all over between them."

The standard 50-minute therapy session was also finished. It was with mixed feelings of relief that I departed from the therapist's office. For better or for worse, memories were being rekindled that I had tried hard to suppress, including another encounter I had with my father. But it would have to wait until my next visit to the clinic...

I gathered my thoughts and picked up where I had last left off.

"After the divorce, my dad moved down to Calgary and got a job as a foreman with the *Canadian Pacific Railway*. He would call us and practically beg my brother William and I to travel there for our summer holidays."

"You don't sound too thrilled at the prospect of spending holidays with your dad," said my therapist.

"We weren't!" I exclaimed. "We were still scared of the man. It was our mom who felt sorry for him and forced us on the *Greyhound* bus bound for 'Cowtown.'

The first night after we arrived, he disappeared and got drunk. The next morning, we awoke to find him passed out on his bed. It was like he couldn't handle the pressure of being a parent, now that we were actually there with him."

"What did you and your brother do then?"

"We didn't know how long he was going to be like that. So we decided to try and entertain ourselves as best we could. We headed down to a nearby trail along the Bow River that our dad had shown us the day before.

There was a train trestle bridge crossing the river to an island on the other side. Being naturally curious kids, that was our destination. So we scampered up the embankment to the bridge above. We stepped carefully on the wooden ties, as we could see beneath our feet the river and exposed rocks far below.

We were about halfway across the bridge, when I looked up and noticed the red signal light at the side of the track had turned green. Because our dad worked for the railway, I had previously asked him how the signals worked. I knew now there was a train coming and we had to get off that bridge as quickly as possible.

Not knowing which direction the train was coming from; I determined that we should push forward. As we quickened our pace, we had to be careful not to get our feet caught between the ties. Being older and bigger than William, I cleared the span first and then cheered him on. Mere moments after he joined me, a train rounded a clump of trees and raced by us."

The therapist smiled, as if he too were cheering us on.

"We waited a few more days for our father to get his act together, but with no luck. So I decided to approach his lair-like bedroom the way you would a bear hibernating in his den and called out his name. He stirred with a grunt. The words marched off my tongue in unison. I spoke of how William and I had come to visit him because he had invited us there, that he had promised to take us to the nearby mountain resort town of Banff, and would he please sober up because we loved him. He said nothing in response. I walked away feeling dejected.

The next day, our dad was up and moving around, acting like nothing had ever happened. My words had somehow penetrated his consciousness after all. William and I knew better than to question him about it. We loaded his car with our suitcases and were off to Banff.

Traveling along the Trans-Canada Highway, entering the rolling Alberta Foothills that connect the sweeping prairie on one side with the imposing Rocky Mountains that tower behind, I marveled out loud at the wondrous sight before us.

Our dad, who had been relatively speechless for most of the drive, came to life and grumbled: 'Pile of rocks! They're nothing but a big pile of rocks!'

Sensing his sour mood, I shut up after that."

The young man opposite me flipped a page in his notebook. "Did you ever miss your father?"

"No," I replied without hesitation. "I mean, any contact we had with the man was usually pretty upsetting. And then when he moved back to Edmonton things got really tense.

An almost foreboding storm had blown into the city on that spring night. Our back screen door at home had been whipped backward by the powerful wind, smashing the glass against the stucco wall. With the wind now howling through the open window and trees rustling in the darkness beyond, my father's face appeared, aptly framed between the remaining pieces of jagged glass.

He asked to stay a few nights, until he could find a place of his own. My mother sympathized, agreeing only to keep the peace.

He eventually moved into the single men's residence of the *Salvation Army* in the inner city; a rough part of town.

One day he called me on the phone. He knew I could use the money and insisted that I come down to skid row immediately and paint a fence around a vacant lot. When I sounded unwilling to venture into that area, he started accusing me of being lazy, good-for-nothing, and lacking ambition. My mother took the phone from me and tried in vain to express our safety concern. I could hear the yelling intensify as it came through the receiver and could only imagine what he was saying. She had no choice but to hang up on him.

About a week later, we heard from my father again. He had begun painting the fence himself, when three thugs approached him demanding money. After he refused their request, they stabbed him between the ribs with a switchblade and left him bleeding. He somehow stumbled his way to get help."

Another therapy session completed. Memories were flying at me from all directions. One stood out among the medley. By this time I was a young man, no longer defenseless against the temperamental outbursts of a tyrannical monster. My beleaguered family, now running on empty, was about to undergo a further turning point...

All Roads Lead to Home

The warm weather confirmed the welcome presence of an Indian summer in 1987. I had earlier mailed away resumes to small town radio stations sprinkled across Western Canada, seeking any available positions as a commercial copywriter, desperate to break free from the ongoing crisis-filled ways of my family. When I received the long distance job offer, my fingers almost ran off a road map trying to pinpoint just exactly where in the wilderness I would be relocating.

The wildest horses you could find in the unbridled province of Alberta couldn't keep me from my dream of a peaceful existence somewhere else. So I proceeded to load my subcompact car 'Pokey' with everything I would need for this expedition through the wilds of northern British Columbia. Sealing the lid on the crammed *U-Haul* rooftop trailer with a padlock, I was gone.

Heading down the highway through the untamed B.C. Interior, it wasn't unusual to be the only vehicle on the road for long stretches, passing road signs warning: "No services – next 150 kilometers."

I would converse with 'Pokey,' my mechanical Sherpa guide, reminding him that I was depending on his Japanese engineering not to let me down now. Inserting one cassette tape after another, playing the same songs repeatedly until I could recite the lyrics from memory, I was intent on staying alert and seizing this career opportunity to start over.

Just when I thought that all civilization had disappeared from the face of the earth, my final destination appeared oasis-like before me. Vast plumes of smoke belched from pulp and paper mills, blanketing this northern town in a thick yellow shroud. Logging trucks rumbled back and forth, carrying formerly proud trees stacked so long and high. I imagined a land of giants, where these hewn logs would be used for leisurely games of *Pick-Up Sticks*.

A sense of unease began to settle in about me. Something didn't feel right, now that I was here. Oh well, it was time to check in with my new employer. The "middle-of-the-road" radio station was really more the middle of nowhere in this remote outpost of humanity. My boss, whom I had never met in person, had promised to find me a place to live in by the time I arrived. After all, it wasn't like I could just move into the local *Holiday Inn* or the Backwoods *Hilton* in the meantime.

To my dismay, there had been nothing done other than a brief posting on the office bulletin board requesting a spare room for me. With limited accommodation in the town, a suggestion that a forgotten old log cabin in the woods might be available for my habitation sent me off on a new search. Upon discovering the isolated cabin, even my youthful desire for adventure couldn't overcome visions of sharing an outhouse with my new neighbors – the Bigfoot family.

I checked into a seedy motel later that night, contemplating what my next move would be. With only cold running water in the bathroom, poor TV reception, and noisy logging trucks racing by my dusty window, the feeling of apprehension grew stronger. I was not meant to be here. Something required my attention back home.

The next morning, I scrawled a short resignation letter to my boss, gave 'Pokey' a hasty inspection, and blew out of town like the wind that whistled through the immense forest surrounding me. I was in such a hurry that I narrowly missed a moose, emerging from the shadows of a frosty dawn, crossing the road ahead. At that point, all I needed was a Mountie on horseback to round the next bend and the average tourist's image of pure Canadiana would have been complete.

By early afternoon, the sun was shining bright on the ribbon of pavement below. Ignoring all speed limit signs, endless tree-filled tracts and distant mountain vistas passed monotonously by, with the reflective glint of an occasional car visible on the horizon. Having not slept very well the previous night, my drowsy eyes became fixated on the centerline of the highway. Eventually I surrendered all consciousness and began to nod off. The refreshing sleep felt so satisfying to my exhausted body.

Out of the blue, I felt an abrupt push from behind, like someone had physically grabbed my shoulders and given me a shake. I raised my head and opened my eyes, only to find that 'Pokey' had crossed the centerline. We were now in the oncoming lane cresting a valley, with two vehicles approaching from below. With mere seconds to react before it was too late, 'Pokey' and I pulled back into the right lane and continued on our trek.

The Prodigal Son returned to Edmonton, another escape attempt foiled. With the revelation of my concerned mother praying for my safe deliverance the same day I fell asleep at the wheel, I soon realized why it was so important that I be at home right now. My father was about to visit his doctor for a standard checkup and the news wouldn't be good. Before long, family circumstances would be dramatically altered again, with me reassuming my "best supporting role" as the dutiful eldest son.

My final visit with the therapist would prove even more enlightening...

Daddy Dearest 2

The probing questions began almost immediately. "What did your father eventually die from?"

"He was diagnosed with inoperable lung cancer due to smoking and would die from it five months later," I said. "We always thought that it would be the alcohol that would finally get him. He had such an addictive personality. My mother used to say that the man smoked like a chimney, drank like a fish, and lied like a sidewalk."

"Tell me about those five months leading up to his death. What was that like?"

"Well, it was stressful, to say the least. No one, including my father, wanted to admit that he was dying. We all naively thought that if he quit smoking and changed his diet, maybe he could beat this thing. But it was too late for that.

I remember visiting him in the hospital one day after he'd been given a wheelchair to get around in. I asked him if he ever used it and he stubbornly said no. I immediately sat down in it and began to wheel myself around his room, trying to convince him of how easy it was to operate. It was of no use; he wasn't interested.

Glancing out the open door into the hallway beyond, I noticed this spry old lady scurrying up and down the hallway as quickly as she could, never stopping to rest.

I asked my dad who this curious character was. He said that everyone there called her the 'Roadrunner.' In a vain attempt to extract laughter from my father, I abruptly turned the wheelchair around and headed out the door. I joined the 'Roadrunner' as she was passing by. With an imaginary finish line at the end of the corridor, the race was on.

The 'Roadrunner' was not amused with her new competition and promptly disappeared into a room on the way. It was worth it, though, to hear my father laughing for the first time in a long while."

My therapist had ceased writing and was now smiling. "It sounds like your relationship with your father was beginning to improve."

"Not really. We just avoided talking about the past, that's all. Until one night…"

I stopped talking and sat motionless, as the memory of that fateful evening flooded my mind.

"I was speaking with the pastor of the church my family was attending at the time. He knew about my father's health condition and was aware of our family's history. So when he asked me if I'd made peace with my father, I was taken aback. I hadn't even thought about it.

But he persisted, going so far as to say that in addition to me forgiving my father; I had to ask him to forgive me for my feelings of anger that I'd been harboring toward him all those years. This really challenged my pride. Needless to say, it wasn't going to be an easy thing for me to do.

I immediately started looking for a way out of this. You know, 'fight or flight.' I protested, saying that by the time I could possibly get to the hospital, visiting hours would be over. The pastor wasn't going to buy that excuse from me and said I may never have this opportunity again.

It wasn't long before I was on my hectic way driving to the hospital. Upon entering my father's room that night, he appeared to be sleeping. He was being pumped full of high doses of morphine to kill the pain and was no longer able to talk.

I almost turned around and left, thinking this was my chance for a quick getaway, but something told me to speak. My father's eyes slowly opened. I began to forgive him for all those terrible years he had put us through and then asked him to forgive me for my feelings of bitterness. I knew that he understood me when he gathered what energy he had left and stretched out his hand for me to shake.

That would be the last time I would see my father alive. He would die three days later."

Like a sudden rainstorm in a parched desert, tears streamed down my face. I now realized that my father's battles had become my own.

Once again refusing my therapist's offer of the strategically placed box of tissues, I wanted to experience those cleansing tears for as long as I could.

More Beddings
and a Funeral

I t was April 1988, and to no one's surprise, my father had died virtually penniless. Now we had his funeral to plan for. If you think it's expensive living in this world today, try departing from it. Our latest challenge would have us see just how economical we could be in this undertaking with the undertaker.

Realizing the ongoing health condition of our younger brother, my sister and I assumed responsibility for all of the arrangements. We set out the next day to tour funeral homes to check on the costs involved, wondering if they ever had sales at these establishments and were there any package deals available? I had to keep reminding myself that we weren't comparing time-share condominiums here.

We were quickly educated at the first business we visited by an unflappable young man. He calmly escorted us through a showroom of neatly arranged coffins on display. Our quest was beginning to take on overtones of new car shopping when he introduced us to the luxurious "*Cadillac* of caskets." A person could have set up camp and lived in that thing, let alone die and be buried in it.

Upon voicing the price range of what we could afford, our tour guide skillfully steered us toward the bargain end of the showroom. With his commission evaporating as we spoke, the salesman suggested that we should consider cremation of the body after the funeral service was over. We could still have a coffin for the actual ceremony, but it would just be a more basic model.

Agreeing with this approach, we were now ushered downstairs to the basement to view the selection of urns available for cremation. We entered what looked like an old wine cellar, with shelf upon shelf containing a potpourri of burial urns. After inquiring as to what would be the least expensive option among this myriad of marble, the salesman responded by handing me a black *Tupperware* container. Thinking he must be joking, I handed it to Dianne and asked who would ever want their remains placed in such a thing.

It was then that he advised us to be careful handling it, because someone's ashes were already inside. It became an instant hot potato, being passed back and forth between us. Apparently, no one had ever returned to claim that particular makeshift urn and its contents.

In This Corner...

T he night before the big event, we had arranged to have a public viewing of the body at the funeral home. My father's "country bumpkin" cousin and his wife decided to stop by my mother's place prior to the viewing. We mistakenly thought it was going to be a sympathy visit, until the rural relative began to speak.

"You people are nothing but a bunch of atheists!" he shouted at us.

According to him, having a closed-casket ceremony at the church the next day was pure sacrilege. Feeling outraged at his ignorant comments, I walked over and confronted him at our back door.

"How dare you come in here and tell us such a thing on a night like this. Who do you think you are?"

His stoical wife intervened by pushing her husband, with arms now flailing, out the door and down the sidewalk.

We arrived at the funeral home not long after that. At his better half's urging, the "country bumpkin" was waiting to apologize for his irrational outburst earlier. I accepted his apology without hesitation, if only to get the man out of my face. It was just in time, as an employee stepped forward to announce that the immediate family could now view the body in private, before any unexpected mass stampede might occur.

Walking somberly down the long hallway toward a secluded room in the back, I rounded the corner to see the coffin with lid open showing my father facing the ceiling. Aside from his lack of hair, due to the recent radiation treatments for cancer, he appeared quite youthful lying there. My mother remarked that he looked almost like he did on their wedding day. I assumed that was meant as a compliment.

The funeral service the next day was a poignant event. There were people present that we hadn't seen in many years. Some of them had steadfastly avoided all contact with us once my parent's marriage dissolved. I didn't know if that was because they were taking sides in the ensuing furor or if they just didn't want to get involved. No matter, they were all there now.

Our church minister opted to be truthful in his remarks, talking realistically about my father's violent life and how he had not only lived by the sword, but eventually died by it as well. There were no minced words to be heard, no need to beat around the worn-out old bush.

Unlike some eulogies where you are left wondering about the deceased person's true identity, no one would have been mistaken about whose funeral they were attending here. In the end, it turned out to be a solemn celebration of a life lived, rather than the mourning of a depressing death.

Earnings, Yearnings, and Urns

U pon going through some of my father's meager belongings the following week, we discovered a receipt for a bank safety deposit box. We determined that he was not the kind of man who would spend good money renting such a high-security device without a valid reason. Visions of all sorts of hidden treasures and mysterious secrets lurking in a sealed metal box danced in our heads. Unable to find the key to its contents only encouraged us even more on our road to its discovery.

Standing in the bank vault a few days later with my sister, the bank manager and a locksmith, we discussed our mission. With our approval, the locksmith began drilling through the thick metal casing, as curious bank customers peered inside to see what all the noise was about. The suspense reached a climax with the bank manager presenting the slender box to us. Removing the lid, our collective balloons would deflate simultaneously, with nothing more than yellowed immigration and divorce papers being revealed.

With no one volunteering to place "dear old dad" on his or her mantle, we decided to bury the urn out in the rural cemetery where his mother had previously been laid to rest. His other country cousin, brother to the open-casket fanatic, maintained the little cemetery on the hill by cutting grass and digging new graves in his spare time. He would have his backhoe warmed up, anxiously awaiting our appearance.

The actual burial would be a very private affair, with only a handful of the closest relatives in attendance. The local minister provided a brief sermon, upon which he gingerly placed the urn in the shallow grave. We each said our final farewells. Not letting any grass grow beneath our feet, the caretaker cousin began scooping black dirt back in to cover the hole he had dug earlier.

Without any available funds after the funeral service was paid for, we decided to postpone purchasing a tombstone for the gravesite. We figured our father wasn't going anywhere in the meantime and would certainly understand our financial predicament in this matter. But as the saying goes, life happens while you're busy making other plans.

Better Late Than Never

F ive years later in 1993, during an economic downturn related to Alberta's boom-or-bust energy industry, I would find myself unemployed and in a restless mood for change. I imagined an exciting job in a faraway place.

Thinking that maybe it was time to take care of any unfinished business at home first, the biggest loose end that still needed tying was my father's unmarked grave. My family agreed that we should return to his final resting place with some kind of permanent marker for it.

After shopping around to find an economically priced tombstone, Dianne, her fiancé, and myself headed out of town on our mission. In an effort to save even more money, we would endeavor to erect the mini-monument ourselves, trying our best not to impersonate *The Three Stooges* at the same time.

It was a blustery afternoon in late October, when we finally descended on the rustic graveyard in Dianne's future husband's pickup truck. With intermittent flakes of snow blowing on a biting cold wind, we unloaded the necessary gear for the noble task that lay before us.

The only problem was that we had forgotten exactly where on this little patch of earth we had buried the urn containing the precious remains half a decade earlier. Feeling like intrepid explorers who had just waded ashore on some remote island, we began to anxiously scour the grassy hill, in search of our hidden treasure.

I briefly contemplated renting a metal detector and scanning the grounds for human mineral deposits. Ruling that theory implausible, I envisioned us pacing up and down the rows with divining rods specially converted for such a task. Maybe we could all join hands and host an impromptu séance to contact the dearly departed for directions. Bring on Larry, Curly, and Moe.

Realizing that my father's original burial place had to have been near his mother's gravesite, we narrowed it down to that vicinity. However, she had been buried in a full-sized coffin and was closely surrounded by other such residents. A backhoe-sized hole with his little urn in it would have had to fit in between there somehow. We held a quick conference and decided on the most likely of potential sites in which to set up the tombstone. If anything, this entire exercise would serve as a form of all-important closure for me.

Escape from Alberta

Sitting in the departure lounge at the Edmonton International Airport, I couldn't wait to get to Vancouver. I loved the ocean and always felt renewed out at Canada's West Coast. It was my way of recharging my batteries and reinvigorating my spirit, just as it had been for my Grandmother who had moved there from the landlocked prairies not long after I was born. I had gotten to appreciate "Lotus Land," as this Canadian version of California is affectionately known, from visiting her out there on numerous occasions when I was a child.

As is the case with many people who flee to anywhere along the West Coast of North America, the Lower Mainland region of British Columbia is seen as a place of new beginnings for lost souls. "Lotus Land" captivates the national psyche in an almost mythical manner, promising a fresh start to all those who are seeking it.

The milder climate of Vancouver makes it one of the few places in Canada where snow is a foreign entity with rare occurrences, due to the warm "Japan current" that washes ashore there year-round. The tradeoff, and there always is one, is that rain takes over where snow leaves off. It's true that you don't have to shovel rain, as the popular retort goes, but it's also been said that in Vancouver you don't tan, you rust.

With my present state of unemployment staring me in the face and winter about to make its presence known in "wild rose country," it didn't take me long to pack my bags for this one-way journey.

The High Lama, I Presume

Unlike most other big city airports in the early 1990s, Edmonton's seemed to revolve around one plane landing and one taking off with great periods of nothing else happening in between. There were no lineups of taxiing aircraft on runways, no planes in holding patterns waiting to land. So whoever was milling about at the time you were milling about in the terminal building, chances were they would be joining you on your upcoming flight.

I scanned the room and noticed a man that stood out in this assemblage of plaid shirts, blue jeans, and baseball caps like a rose in winter. Wrapped in a flowing wine-colored robe, wearing sandals and with a shaved head, he was a Buddhist monk. This was definitely not a sight you would see very often in this neck of the northern woods. He was probably just as eager as I was for the plane to take off, plucking us both from this hinterland and depositing us in our own personal *Shangri-La*.

I lost sight of him as fellow passengers finally began to board. Heading down the aisle to my assigned seat, I sat down beside a window in excited anticipation. I always liked to see not only where I was leaving from, but also where I was going. It would serve as a form of undeniable confirmation to myself that my latest escape plan was a successful one.

The plane was going to be full as usual, no doubt packed with fleeing escapees like myself. Crammed into this giant metal cigar tube on wheels like the human sardines that we were forced to become, there was one empty seat left on the entire plane, located between myself and a young man by the aisle.

Suddenly the Buddhist monk entered the cabin and strolled in my direction. *Oh great,* I thought to myself. *Now I can spend the next one and a half hours listening to someone preach to me his religion, and I bet he hasn't washed that robe in weeks.*

I was instantly reminded of a classic Dave Berg cartoon from *Mad* magazine when I was a teenager. It depicts a conservative businessman sitting on a near-empty bus, when a disheveled guy climbs aboard and starts heading down the aisle toward him. All sorts of negative thoughts proceed to run through the businessman's head. With lots of seats available to sit in, the "bum" who probably hadn't bathed in ages would inevitably choose to sit beside the "suit," undoubtedly hitting him up for money. As it turns out, the homeless fellow walks on by to the back of the bus, leaving Mr. High Society to now wonder why he wasn't good enough to sit beside. This impromptu pre-flight analogy couldn't help but force me to do a quick attitude adjustment and prepare for my new seatmate.

Dusk was rapidly descending upon the surrounding countryside as our plane hurtled down the runway. I leaned back in my seat, watching the airport fade away, silently praying that it would be a safe flight. The monk leaned forward to also check out the view through our little porthole of a window. I pretended not to notice his gaze and wondered if I'd be able to make it through the flight without having to strike up a conversation with him. There were times in my life when I just couldn't wait to meet such a stranger and find out what made him tick. But there were other times that I just wanted to be left alone to my thoughts. This was one of those times.

It is not uncommon to experience turbulence while flying over the snow-capped peaks of the Canadian Rockies. Often the pilot, whether out of tradition or some sort of ritualistic expectation, will leave the "fasten seatbelt" sign on during the entire journey. This flight was no exception, but the turbulence we were about to encounter certainly was.

The flight attendants were busy serving drinks and snacks, when the plane started its roller coaster ride over the Rockies. As if the air pockets we were hitting were coming at us on a giant conveyor belt, we would repeatedly drop and then rise up again.

I began to think about all things spiritual and wondered what my monkish neighbor thought of this wild ride. He was always smiling, so I couldn't adequately gauge his reaction to this latest happening. The young man on the aisle could be heard muttering something about his girlfriend impatiently waiting for him at the Vancouver airport.

I broke my vow of silence and commented to the monk about the bumpy flight. He reassured me that everything would be fine. I jokingly asked him if he knew something about our airborne excursion that I didn't, causing him to laugh. This seemed to be the icebreaker we needed to jumpstart our conversation. It turned out that he was some sort of Master monk criss-crossing North America, teaching new monks in the ways of Buddhism. He was also a former Hong Kong businessman in his pre-enlightened days, producing a photo ID card showing his previously hair-covered head wearing a three-piece suit to prove it.

By now I was oblivious to the air turbulence buffeting our flying cigar tube. The young man on the aisle reiterated his hope that Mother Nature's unplanned in-flight entertainment wouldn't delay our landing, so as to appease his anxious girlfriend.

The Master monk then invited me to visit the Vancouver temple where he was currently based. With that said, our plane descended through a cloud bank, revealing the forested contours of the Gulf Islands sitting atop a shimmering glass palette that was the Pacific Ocean. We had once again found our respective *Lost Horizon*.

In My Father's Shadow

I t was New Year's Eve, 1994, and I had to deliver a rental deposit to my new landlord in a suburb of Vancouver. If I didn't meet the deadline in time, my new bachelor pad would become the property of one of the many other recent arrivals in town. Not being as familiar with the outskirts of town, I boarded a city bus and rode it for what seemed like forever on that rainy night.

I was wet and hungry by the time I found the address I was looking for. My landlord invited me inside his palatial home to help celebrate the festive occasion with a generous drink of *Southern Comfort*. One toast led to another toast and yet another, with me almost forgetting why I was there. I decided that I should hand over the check and make my exit before I might say or do something I would later regret.

Once back outside, I stumbled down the rain-polished sidewalk and up the darkened street. Where was I anyhow? Everything looked so different at night. I hadn't eaten anything since earlier in the day, so the booze took effect quickly. I was so happy at the thought of my newfound freedom, that I seemed impervious to the sleet that was striking me now.

Noticing the lights of motor vehicle traffic in the distance, I aimed my fatigued body in the direction of where I thought the bus would travel.

Standing at the bus stop near the curb, I was soaked to the bone, in part by passing vehicles that almost seemed to be going out of their way to ensure there wasn't a dry patch left on my person. I laughed giddily, for nothing could ruin this night. Busses would pass me by, one after another in succession, without stopping to pick me up. Could it have something to do with the fact that I looked like a giant wet rat?

About two hours later, finally sober enough to make a clear observation of my surroundings, I looked more closely at what I thought was the bus stop. It turned out to really be nothing more than a scrawny tree in disguise. After having promised myself to never follow in my alcoholic father's footsteps, I had just experienced my first drunken escapade. It wouldn't be my last.

One Last Chance

The basement suite I moved into wasn't really convenient for someone with my six-foot-two frame. I would be painfully reminded to duck my tender head upon entering the low-ceilinged living room and avoided using that area because of it. With only a flat piece of foam for sleeping on, a folding chair for sitting, and a single plate, cup, knife, fork, and spoon for eating, I quickly chose to be out of my new apartment more than I was in.

The days of unemployment and searching for a job blurred into weeks and then a couple of months. I was living off of borrowed money and credit. Paying my credit card bills by taking out credit card cash advances was giving new meaning to the term "trickle-down economics." I would give myself a few more days of trying to find gainful employment, before giving up on my dream of putting down roots in "Lotus Land" once and for all.

Scanning "help wanted" ads in the newspaper one day, I proceeded to write out my quota of cover letters and package them with their corresponding resumes. Dropping them off at the nearest mailbox a few hours later, I glanced down to pick up the latest edition of a community paper. Flipping through the pages, my attention was drawn to an ad for customer service representatives required at a new *Kinko's Copy Center* that was about to open. I debated whether to bother applying for it. After all, I had already sent out numerous other resumes. Surely one of those employers would respond with positive news.

By the time I got back home, my mind was made up. I was desperate to find work. What harm could it do to reply to yet one more ad that day? As it turned out, only *Kinko's* called for an interview and offered me full-time employment within days. Working there would be both a blessing and a curse for me. But more than anything, it would enable me to remain out at the West Coast.

Starting a job at the only *Kinko's* location in town at the time was similar to joining the colony of worker bees in a giant hive. Being the eternal night owl that I am, I enlisted in the all-male night crew working the 4:00 pm to 12:30 am shift.

The sour night supervisor was a caricature of Moe, the hard-boiled bartender from *The Simpsons*. It wouldn't take long before he would notice my lack of technical prowess and banish me from ever operating the big equipment. He actually took his foot and drew an invisible line on the floor around any machinery larger than a filing cabinet, forbidding me from crossing over. I was ordered to do what I did best and provide customer service at the front counter instead.

I used to say that sooner or later everyone would have to visit our *Kinko's.* With a prime location on busy West Broadway and being open 24 hours a day, seven days a week, customers came from far and wide. It was like we were the only game in town.

Diverse clientele such as famous actors working in the bustling Vancouver film industry, local politicians hot on the campaign trail, small business owners struggling to stay afloat, assorted psychics at large, and university students pulling all-nighters could be seen hurrying through our doors.

Human nature being what it is, many of these eclectic customers would leave whatever they needed done to the last minute. Expecting us to drop everything and put everyone else's latest emergency on hold for their urgent request, I often felt like I'd assumed a position at the United Nations Security Council. We even made the list of a local newspaper's annual reader's survey rating the best places in Vancouver to witness people "freaking out." Listed right behind the frenzied International Airport was our good old *Kinko's*.

There was such camaraderie amongst the staff, day and night shifts combined, that people frequenting the store viewed it as a sort of meeting place. With a collection of employees that were truly international in their origin, it looked as though management had set up a recruiting booth outside the immigration office, literally hiring people as they stepped off the boat.

But it was that multicultural mix of co-workers, attracting similarly curious customers, who added the element of eccentricity to what would have been an otherwise dull establishment. I mean, a person can only photocopy so many people's resumes (Will that be on laid or linen bond?), fax so many documents (Would you like a cover page with that?), and clear so many photocopier paper jams (#%$&@!?) before their mind begins to atrophy.

The store vibrated with activity like a perpetual war zone. Upon entering the battlefield at 4:00 pm every day, the sound of photocopiers humming, the acrid smell of toner permeating the air, and the sight of countless bodies scurrying back and forth would greet me. I was one of the reinforcements, arriving for the changing of the guard, allowing the exhausted day troops to get some much-needed "R & R."

It became routine to deal with irate customers on a nightly basis, whose questioning and complaining about things could often be quite inane. In a busy and demanding retail environment such as *Kinko's,* the hardworking staff couldn't help but develop a strong bond between themselves, reminiscent of veterans in an ongoing war.

Late Blooming Boomer

I t was in this group of assorted co-workers that I first met Mark. The sparks bounced off each of us like hailstones on a metal roof whenever we worked together. I was the complete antithesis of him and everything he represented. He was the Oscar Madison to my Felix Unger in our West Coast rendition of *The Odd Couple.* But to everyone's astonishment, proving yet again that opposites attract, Mark and I would become new best friends.

Unlike many people working for the same employer, who just want to get away from each other at the end of their shift, Mark and I couldn't wait till our days off to celebrate "guys night out" together. We would head over to a neighborhood video store, rent whatever "guys" action movies were popular, stop by the liquor store to purchase beer for Mark and wine coolers for my more refined palate, then descend upon my place to order pizza delivery. It would be a night of purely immature and drunken frivolity, your typical male fraternity scene on campus. But for me it would mean so much more. For the first time ever, I truly felt like "one of the boys."

Our "frat house" antics varied from week to week, but were fast becoming legend at *Kinko's*. One night, we settled on the old standard of water balloons. I had recently moved into an apartment on the fourth floor. With a balcony included, the stage was set.

After launching a volley of balloons and not accomplishing anything other than washing the street below, the situation quickly changed. An innocent victim had appeared out of nowhere and dared to walk in the path of one of our oncoming projectiles.

Understandably, this person was none too happy at taking an unexpected shower late at night. Grumbling at this man-made cloudburst, they vanished into the darkness, while we recoiled in laughter.

The evening progressed and more balloons were launched. All at once, three police cars pulled up in front of our building.

"They're entering the lobby," yelled Mark.

"Destroy all the evidence!" I called back.

Like a well-trained commando in one of our action videos, Mark crawled on his stomach out onto the balcony. Throwing our supply of unused ammunition back into the living room, I collected the evidence and ran to the kitchen. Grabbing a butcher knife, I replayed the infamous moment from the movie *Psycho* in my mind. "Pop, pop, pop," went the balloons. "Bang, bang, bang," went the door.

"Open up! This is the police!"

"Quick, pretend like you were sleeping," I whispered.

Running to my bedroom, I stripped to a T-shirt and boxer shorts. My partner in crime rushed to the other bedroom and while fully clothed, hopped into bed. Opening the door to my apartment, I wiped my eyes and squinted as if I'd just been awakened from a deep slumber.

"What's the matter?" I innocently inquired.

Two police officers stood at attention before me.

"You know perfectly well why we're here. We're investigating an assault and battery with water bombs!"

The officers brushed by me and then my roommate's curious black cat Hugo, abruptly jumping out of their path. One officer began to tour the apartment, apparently looking for anything remotely suspicious. He then discovered my friend pretending to sleep.

"Come out here!" he summoned.

Playing the game of "good cop/bad cop," the other officer had to keep turning away so we wouldn't see him cracking up with laughter. His gruff partner fired the questions at us.

"Why were you two throwing water bombs? Don't you think you're a little old for this?"

Mark stood speechless. I just stood in my underwear.

"We haven't admitted to doing anything," I answered defiantly.

"Oh, come on! This isn't the O.J. Simpson case. There's no missing glove to be found here," the serious officer replied.

At that remark, the rest of us could no longer contain ourselves and open laughter ensued.

"Don't deny it," he persisted. "We saw your curtains move. We heard voices in here."

All I could say was, "Well, we do have a cat." Hugo looked on, assuming his new role as scapegoat in stride.

"Oh, and your cat can talk, can he?" came the sarcastic response.

You don't know Hugo, I thought to myself. We finally gave in and admitted to our dastardly deed.

"Now don't you feel embarrassed?" asked one of the officers.

Looking down at my colorful boxer shorts, I was embarrassed. We apologized and agreed to never again throw water balloons—at least not from my apartment.

As the police departed, I wondered what would have happened if the night had been any slower for the "boys in blue." We might have had the local SWAT team, helicopters hovering overhead, scaling the side of our building instead.

On another occasion, Mark and I decided to take our act on the road. It happened to be a few days after Halloween. I had graduated to using a corkscrew and sipping red wine by now, while Mark gulped down his usual beer. Knowing my tendency to become the "life-of-the-party" when having drank too much, my generous friend made sure that my wine glass was quickly refilled every time I turned around. He couldn't wait to find out what our next comedic mission would be.

With the arrival home of my disapproving roommate, I abruptly rose to my feet.

"Let's blow this joint!" I proclaimed.

Leaving my relieved roommate behind, Mark and I headed out the door of my apartment building and down the street. The trendy Kitsilano neighborhood was dotted with grand old Victorian-style homes. But I spotted something else in common amongst these stately residences. Almost every house had a plump jack-o'- lantern left over from recent Halloween festivities, sitting proudly on display on an open veranda.

Without ever mentioning my intention, I crept up on the first front porch we came to. Grabbing the giant pumpkin in my hands, I hoisted the orange gourd above my head. I must have looked like an inebriated Atlas, holding a topsy-turvy world on my shoulders.

Mark started to laugh as I staggered down the sidewalk, determined not to drop my precious cargo. Upon reaching the boulevard out front, I gathered all of my strength and hurled the globe-like object through the air. We watched as the pumpkin smashed unceremoniously on the black asphalt, creating a pockmark-like impression.

We continued this activity down the street and onto the next block, both of us taking turns at smashing pumpkins. Residents seemed completely unaware of what was going on, probably expecting such capers to have been performed during the actual night of All Hallows' Eve.

It was my turn once again, standing imperiously atop another front porch, my trophy held aloft like I had just won the Super Bowl. All of a sudden, Mark yelled to me that a man inside the house had seen us and was heading our way. I hurried down the stairs, careful not to release my prized possession before it was time, tripping on one of the bottom steps in my haste.

My right foot felt awkward, but I managed to crawl over the front fence, all the time refusing to let go of the pumpkin. The latest missile went flying through the air, completing an erratic pattern of orange-colored craters on the street that resembled an urban air raid in progress. I was now dragging one leg as

I walked, looking like the stereotypical monster from an old horror movie. Numbed to the pain that was throbbing in my injured foot, I struggled to keep up with Mark.

It wasn't long before I could no longer keep pace and since it was getting late anyways, we decided to call it a night. My senses were still dulled from having drank a full bottle of wine earlier. I said good-bye to Mark and retired to my bed, thinking that I must have just sprained my foot. Not until the next morning, when I would rise to go to the bathroom and drop to the floor in agony, did I realize the injury was more serious.

Sitting in a hospital Emergency room a few hours later, surrounded by toughened football and rugby players sporting more manly injuries acquired during their latest game, I chose to remain silent when asked how I wound up there. X-rays would reveal a fractured bone in my badly swollen right foot. The accompanying crutches would be a gentle reminder to my *Kinko's* co-workers of our latest adventure. As absurd as it may sound, though, I was having fun.

There was something very nostalgic propelling two adult men to pursue these seemingly juvenile pranks. For Mark, it was a chance to relive his youth and the fun-filled memories that went with it. For me, it was a golden opportunity to experience the youth that I had inadvertently skipped over. I could now relate to what I had only overheard my peers talk about during my high school days 15 years earlier.

Being a late bloomer in most things that other young men had already experienced as a rite of passage had become my style. The fact that I had never been drunk until I was in my early thirties and living in Vancouver was proof of that. The fact that my father had been an alcoholic, and as his son I was at risk of inheriting a genetic predisposition toward becoming addicted to alcohol also, was not lost on me. I just had to remind myself of it periodically.

It's My Party, and I'll Die If I Want To

Where had I been, where did I want to go, and why? Confronting these pertinent questions was like opening my very own "Pandora's box." My on-again, off-again state of depression only intensified, with ever-changing mood swings becoming the norm for me. It was time to get some professional help.

The General Practitioner I was seeing wanted a second opinion concerning my mental health. After all, I could be on top of the world, the resident "life-of-the-party" one evening, and in the depths of suicidal despair the next morning. The only thing predictable about these fluctuating mood swings within me was that they were unpredictable. It was becoming increasingly difficult for me to keep personal commitments and to maintain enthusiasm. The doctor recommended I meet with a specialist at the historic St. Paul's Hospital near downtown.

My big fear was that if people knew the real me, they would never want to speak to me again. Was I nothing but a big phony for appearing friendly and outgoing in person, yet despondent and withdrawn when alone? These opposing sides of my personality, completely genuine and valid on their own, felt like they were going to tear me apart from within.

After meeting privately with the head psychiatrist in his office, he invited me to move to a more sterile-looking room with only two chairs and a large glass mirror on the wall beside. I was then introduced to a student who was training in psychiatry. My permission was requested to allow a group of similar students to sit in a room on the other side of what was actually a one-way mirrored window to observe our discussion. The head of psychiatry would join them, leaving us alone to have our so-called "one-on-one" conversation. This arrangement might have been daunting, if not for my urgent need to find out what was wrong with me.

When all was said and done, it was confirmed that I was suffering from Bipolar Disorder, the new face on the old bogeyman known as manic-depression. There was a twist, though, in that I resided within a minority of this minority in the human population. My form of depression had been narrowed down to specifically Bipolar Disorder—Type 2, Rapid Cycling. This elaborate title described the frequently changing nature of my mood swings. Unlike most people battling the more common variety of this disorder and how their moods could take many weeks or months to alternate between, mine could transform from night to day.

The extreme states of manic elation, experienced when I was feeling up, could be risky at times. It was not uncommon for money to "burn a hole in my pocket" with me buying or doing things during these emotional highs, that I would never have seriously considered otherwise. One such incident happened when I headed off, with normal inhibitions in retreat, once more...

Like Diamonds,
Tattoos are Forever

Sixteen steps up a flight of stairs. That's all that stood between me and my plan to get a tattoo. I climbed the stairs slowly, pondering my decision with every step. Would I live to regret this in the future? And what would my family and friends think? In their eyes, I was too moderate a person to engage in such a "wild" act.

Upon entering the tattoo parlor, I heard the familiar buzzing sound synonymous with such establishments. In one room, a multi-colored butterfly was making a permanent landing above a young lady's bellybutton.

I sat down with anticipation and started flipping through stacks of binders filled with a variety of designs. You name it; they had it. And if they didn't have exactly what you were looking for, they would custom-design it.

My dream tattoo was of a blue dolphin. But there would be no cartoon characters for me. Flipper would have to wait. I turned the page and there he was, a stylish tribal dolphin from

South America. As if visiting an animal shelter, I decided to adopt this new pet and take him home with me.

A young man reminding me of Johnny Depp approached. He assured me he would have no problem reproducing the design on my chest. We chatted for a while, forming a sort of doctor-patient relationship with each other. Then it was time.

We entered the room where it would all happen. Colorful photographs of previous customer's tattoos adorned the walls, while broad ceiling fans whirled overhead. I felt magically transported to some exotic locale, reminiscent of a scene from *The Night of the Iguana*.

I removed my shirt and sat down. We decided where the outline should be placed on my chest and the area was then shaved. I held my breath as the "doctor" unwrapped the first needle he would use to puncture and insert pigment in my skin. Realizing that irregular breathing patterns might cause my sleek dolphin to look more like a humpback whale, I made a conscious effort to relax.

The following 90 minutes would see my dolphin grow from the tail up. I had been captivated with these sea creatures and their playful, yet intelligent ways since I was a little boy. This would be my lasting tribute to them, I thought.

The indelibly inked blue dolphin that presently leaps off of my right pectoral is classy enough, but probably wouldn't have swam my way in the first place, if not for me being so elated at that particular moment.

Other areas in my life adversely affected by this condition included virtually anything that I would undertake requiring enthusiasm. It didn't matter whether I was signing up for a school course, starting a new job, beginning a friendship, or learning a hobby. The initial feelings of excitement and energy couldn't be maintained for long, with me losing interest like a slowly leaking flat tire. To follow through on anything with anyone was fast becoming a challenge.

Talented singer-songwriter Joni Mitchell, when describing her own experience dealing with the broader form of this illness, once said: "Depression can be the sand that makes the pearl."

Other well-known sufferers, who produced their own pearls of wisdom, included such eminent statesmen as Abraham Lincoln and Winston Churchill. These larger-than-life figures battled this malady tirelessly throughout their careers, managing to leave their accomplished imprints on world history during times of great upheaval.

Now that I had the right medical diagnosis, the next step would be to find the proper medication. After trying various antidepressants, weighing their particular side effects versus benefits, my doctor and I settled on an anticonvulsant that was more suitable for dealing with erratic mood swings. This helped somewhat in the restoration of emotional equilibrium within me.

Over time, I was able to recognize these depressive bouts for what they were, along with a pattern concerning how long the average episode would last. To my relief, I have learned that no matter how dark things may appear at any particular moment, the negative mood in question will pass within a few days.

This enduring emotional struggle couldn't help but remind me of my friend Mark's befitting motto: "You have to experience the bad, in order to appreciate the good."

Feeling regenerated, I began my search for a new job. Due to Vancouver being the embarkation point for the burgeoning Alaska-bound cruise ship industry, Canadians were encouraged to apply for a wide variety of employment on board.

I was interviewed and subsequently hired for a new life at sea, to be based initially in the Caribbean. After having quit my present job twice before, it would be "three time's the charm," as I gladly delivered a letter of resignation to my boss at *Kinko's*.

Quest for Hair

Something else had contributed to my current state of depression, going back to when I was 23 years old. An ever-widening part in my hair had appeared. I was going bald!

There are a number of stages a man goes through when he makes this fateful discovery: shock, panic, desperation. The first thing I did was to see my dermatologist. After all, I was a rational man and there had to be a logical approach to this. It was confirmed; I had male-pattern baldness.

Have you ever noticed how there are some people who feel it is their duty to point out the obvious to you? For instance, there was the hair stylist who asked if I knew that I was losing my hair. It was as if I didn't own a mirror.

Suddenly, all those magazine ads for hair loss remedies from my youth came to mind. You know, the ones placed between: "You too can grow Sea Monkeys" and "Let Charles Atlas help you visit the beach again!"

I remember calling one company in Texas that had made wonderful claims. They could grow real hair, and had the before and after pictures to prove it. A good ole' boy with a Slim Pickens kind-of-voice answered the phone. When he found out

I was from Canada, he declared: "Son, with what we've got in this here tonic, they wouldn't let it past your border!"

It sounded more like a new fuel.

I'd better try something closer to home. I noticed a newspaper ad boasting how acupuncture could grow hair. Leave it to the ancient Chinese—this had to be legitimate.

It wasn't long before I found myself lying on a table, an acupuncturist inserting needles in my scalp. Then came the worst part—my bony ankles and wrists. But for ultimate effectiveness, the needles had to be connected with wires to a live battery on a nearby cart. I must have looked like Dr. Frankenstein's latest creation, but it would all be worth it in my quest for hair.

I returned there on a weekly basis. During one visit, all hooked up and dreaming of how new locks were sprouting by the minute, a jolt of electricity abruptly shot through my body. After practically peeling myself off the ceiling, the acupuncturist revealed that she had been having problems with the battery lately. I was told not to worry, since the electric surge would do wonders for my circulation. I didn't think so and promptly left.

There was another local business extolling the breakthroughs it had made battling baldness. All I had to do was buy a monthly supply of their miracle formula, apply it to my scalp every night, and come in for a weekly treatment. I was guaranteed that in no time at all, I'd look like I played in a rock band.

Sitting in the waiting room with other young and balding men, at least I didn't feel alone in my plight. We could have formed our own therapy group, but would have needed a similarly "follicle-challenged" therapist to guide us.

Back at home, while eagerly rubbing the new hair lotion on my bald spot, my mother was busy baking in the kitchen nearby. She had run out of cooking oil and was searching for a suitable replacement. Our eyes met as we both realized my secret potion would probably do more good in her cake than on my head.

Maybe I'd been looking too hard for a solution and couldn't see the hair for the peach fuzz. There must have been something I'd overlooked. I recalled a classmate from my college days that had suggested he would simply shave his head if ever faced with this problem. The hair was sure to grow back in twice as thick.

The timing of such a daring act, done long before the trendy hairstyle that it is today, would have to be just right. I waited until I was on holidays and visiting a friend in Toronto. He dropped me off at a local mall to kill time while he ran an errand. I spotted a barbershop and thought: Here's my chance, it's now or never!

When my friend returned half an hour later, shock would be an understatement in describing his reaction to my new look. Shaving my head didn't help my hair condition very much, but it did provide me with an excuse to consider a career in the military.

Arrivals and Departures

I returned to Edmonton in time to spend the Christmas holidays with my family and friends. This temporary stay in my hometown would be a pit stop in my journey; long enough to convert a few items in my luggage from cold to warm weather wear.

If I had wondered whether anything had improved in family relations while I was gone, the latest feud requiring my best efforts in mediation would provide me with my answer. Needless to say, I would look forward to heading off to the Caribbean to report for duty on board the cruise ship, early in the New Year of 1998.

The much-anticipated "El Nino" weather phenomenon was reportedly on its way riding the ocean currents up the Pacific, but had yet to make its warming appearance to winter-weary dwellers in Western Canada. The January morning that I carried my luggage out to the waiting taxicab, en route to the airport, was an inhuman 20 degrees below Fahrenheit. I would arrive in a winter-immune San Juan, Puerto Rico, and 90 above temperatures later that evening.

Enjoying a hotel breakfast the next morning, overlooking the ocean liner with other new crewmembers, was exciting. The eight of us had flown in from all over the globe to participate in the first official training program for Junior Officers. The next three weeks would include intensive instruction in basic sea survival, emergency response skills, and cross-training in various shipboard departments.

I would go on to become good friends with a female trainee from Austria. Katharina and I would commiserate together as we found ourselves in situations more akin to basic training for new recruits in military boot camp. Our personal chemistry with each other was such that we would just have to look at the other person in anticipation of their reaction to the latest challenge, and we would burst out laughing in response.

Upon docking at St. Thomas, U.S. Virgin Islands, one day, all Junior Officers were directed to board an old school bus waiting beside the pier. The vehicle looked like it had taken a long detour off the set of the 1970s TV sitcom *The Partridge Family*.

Leaving the exclusive duty-free jewelry shops of the quaint port behind us, the bus wound its way along a highway heading toward the other side of the island. With exotic beaches beckoning in the distance, we turned off the main road and entered the local garbage dump. My overactive imagination convinced me this must be some sort of shortcut to a secluded little island hideaway that the tourist hordes were unaware of. How ingenious, I surmised, to disguise the entrance to this tropical retreat by having us drive through such camouflaged surroundings to get there.

Arriving at the peak of what had to be the most scenic waste management site on the planet, our bus came to a grinding halt. With the sun shining warmly on the aquamarine waters of the Caribbean Sea below, we were instructed to disembark. Surely there must be a path down to the beach from here, I thought, as we gathered outside.

We were now being guided over to a giant fire pit. Maybe they were going to treat us to a complimentary barbeque before we caught some rays on the sandy shores nearby.

Instead, a variety of color-coded fire extinguishers were lined up on the ground before us. Lighting the pit aflame with different accelerants, and then explaining the significance of using the right extinguisher for the corresponding type of blaze, we were expected to avoid turning the adjacent dump into an out-of-control fireball. Taking turns snuffing out the flaming bonfire, I guess roasting marshmallows was out of the question.

We then walked over to a metal shed not far away. Our determined instructor lectured us as to the importance of being able to find our way around an enclosed space in a dark and smoky atmosphere. With visions of a number of existing nightclubs that fit that description dancing in my head, our fearless troop was ushered inside the windowless structure.

Katharina made the comment that this might not have been a good day to wear her white pants after all. I agreed with her assumption, as we were told to drop to our knees and place one hand on the metal wall. Slamming the only door to the darkened building behind him as he promptly departed, our drill sergeant wannabe proceeded to set the exterior of the shed on fire.

We now had to crawl along the inside perimeter, always keeping one hand on the wall beside us for guidance, until we found that all-important door leading to freedom and safety outside. Ignoring the wall that was heating up fast, I grabbed onto Katharina's legs in front of me. Laughing and coughing, we emerged triumphant from another day of Marine Corps training on our very own Parris Island.

Our next attempt at playing *Survivor* would be on the French-speaking island of Martinique the following week. Once again, we boarded a bus and traveled to the interior of the island. We were informed today's lesson would be spent by the pool. I dared to entertain the thought of suntanning my albino-like appearance away, something that is so visibly representative of Canadians at that time of year. Yet again, I would be disappointed.

Upon arriving at an outdoor swimming facility, it was strangely vacant of people. In a scene simulating the mega-hit movie *Titanic,* when the ocean liner was sinking and its lifeboats had been lowered to rescue distraught passengers, we were shown an overturned life raft bobbing in the pool. It was our duty to take turns climbing an Olympic regulation diving tower, jumping off and turning the life raft upright, while assisting people to safely get on board.

Being the last participant to ascend the tower, my legs began to shake as I neared the top. This was no time to experience a fear of heights, I reminded myself, not to mention the minor technicality of my being a poor swimmer. I approached the end of the diving board and closed my eyes tightly. Not knowing how long I was standing there in that petrified state, I was aroused by a chorus of "Jump! Jump! Jump!" arising from a bevy of buoyant bodies in the pool below.

The next thing I knew I was in the water, struggling with the life raft, my long legs tangled in its many lines. The rescuer would need rescuing. It would be everyone for themselves at any cruise ship muster station I was in charge of. (Note to self: don't board any older ships due to greater sinking potential and fear of being doomed.)

The day when our training ended and the new graduates were being dispersed to various other ships in the fleet, my heart sunk as I bid bon voyage to a teary-eyed Katharina who was leaving for another vessel. If misery loves company, we would both need to find new kindred spirits to help us get by now.

Pirate of the Caribbean

L ife on board a cruise ship, which is basically a floating
hotel, is a closely-knit community of people who are
working there for distinct reasons. Some people are escaping
failed careers or relationships on land, seeing this ungrounded
lifestyle as a fresh start or last resort. Others may be more career-
minded about it all.

With the average employee contract on the ship being six
months in duration, there was a steady stream of crewmembers
coming and going. Just as I would get to know a cabin mate,
they would disembark and someone new would take their place.
This nomadic, rootless existence is a way of life on board that
is appreciated by some and resented by others.

The officers of the ships in our fleet were either of British or
Italian origin. If you worked on board a British ship, you were
guaranteed a life of protocol and the class system that went
along with it. Everything was by the book, rules were carved in
stone, and mistakes were not easily tolerated. Conversely, if you
happened to be on board a ship with its Italian counterparts,
life was allegedly one big party, and pretty women had better

beware. I would soon find myself stepping back in time to a more Dickensian era, since mine was a British ship.

Rumors had been circulating for a while that we would be receiving another Junior Officer the next time we docked in Old San Juan. His name was Raj and his reputation definitely preceded him, since he wasn't new to the job, just our specific ship. He was a curious character, originally from India, but with a western twist. Having always appreciated a non-conformist with a wry sense of humor, we would become fast friends onboard.

Our immediate supervisor was an acid-tongued Brit named Cassandra. She was physically short in stature, but then so was Napoleon. Cassandra ran her department like a warden does a state penitentiary. She considered her position as that of a taskmaster, with no room allowed for dissension by anyone. It was "her way or the seaway." In her eyes, we were viewed as a collection of incompetent underlings who were in desperate need of her unique brand of discipline. With my deep-rooted dislike of authority figures that abuse their personal power, I could envision the impending "writing on the wall."

Under Cassandra's watch, we would work long hours, seven days a week. Being cross-trained in a variety of departments, we would often toil in split shifts so as to provide round-the-clock coverage. I realized that an irregular work schedule was the nature of the business before I ever set foot on the ship. But her lack of respect for those in positions beneath her, combined with her tyrannical nature and sadistic desire to make or break us, made the job increasingly unbearable.

Cassandra's standard response to a bleary-eyed Junior Officer deprived of sleep was to: "Quit your whinging!" (the British equivalent of whining).

Recalling the early days of her nautical career, she elaborated further.

"You don't know the meaning of the word 'work' until you've done it for 16 hours in a day."

I suppose that was meant to make us feel better.

Just Don't Call Me 'Gopher'

The first day of any cruise was usually spent entirely at sea. If we were going to experience rough sailing at all, being in open water and far from land would be the time.

Working the front desk was an eye-opening way to see what went on behind the scenes with passengers and employees alike. Depending on the time of shift, I could always count on something unorthodox happening that hadn't quite been covered in the salty sailor's manual during training.

This included everything from a depressed woman threatening to jump into the murky depths in the dead of the night, a sobbing teenaged girl pleading to have her alcoholic mother banned from drinking in the ship's lounges, to a claustrophobic family desperate for a stateroom with a porthole when only an interior cabin was available.

A common question of many passengers was what were my recommendations for the best beaches and other tourist attractions on the various islands that we were scheduled to visit. Not having had the time or opportunity to ever see much outside the actual port we would dock in, I would summon up all of my diplomatic skills and calmly hand the inquiring party a selection of colorful travel brochures.

During one particular cruise, a virulent strain of flu had invaded our ship. It was being spread back and forth between unsuspecting passengers and crewmembers alike. This vicious cycle perpetuated itself with the inadvertent help of sleep-deprived staff whose immune systems were ripe for such a viral attack.

My turn to experience the illness came one night when I awoke to find myself laying in perspiration-soaked bed sheets, sweating profusely on my bunk. Within hours, my hot flashes would be replaced by cold and uncontrollable shivering.

The ship would be arriving in St. Thomas later that morning. Before that happened, I thought I should visit the front desk to see if there was any medicine I could possibly take and to inform my supervisor of my sickly condition.

"Quit your bloody whinging and get to work!"

Cassandra could never be accused of vagueness in her authoritarian response. The fact that I was paler than pale and could barely stand made no difference to her.

I would go on to assist U.S. Immigration by handing out passports to eager passengers so they could disembark the ship, then return to the front desk for my regular duties there, and finally head down to the crew office in order to process more paperwork. It was just another day at sea for me, where standard labor laws didn't apply as long as we were operating in international waters.

As the days passed, it came time for one of Cassandra's dreaded staff meetings. Her idea of motivating employees consisted of going around the room and individually berating them in front of their peers. You could hear the proverbial pin drop at these sessions, with people frozen at grim attention, fearing their turn at the upcoming inquisition.

Not one member of the predominantly English crew would stand up to her petty accusations. When she turned her "evil eye" to myself, to my amazement, she offered no criticism. Instead, she made the mistake of asking for my opinion on how staff morale could be improved.

I briefly contemplated the matter, took a deep breath, and replied that many of us found her to be unapproachable when we needed her help. Cassandra was speechless. Had no one dared to question her actions to her face before?

After the "kangaroo court" was adjourned, co-workers approached me to offer their silent support and explain their fear of confronting our female Captain Bligh.

Raj's cliché-styled response was characteristically altered: "Let barking dogs bark! You know what I mean? Let barking dogs bark!"

I couldn't believe this English aversion to "making waves," so to speak, and their steadfast adherence to this outdated hierarchical class system. Human rights had been effectively torpedoed on the high seas and sunk to the level of an oxymoron.

My own maternal grandfather had emigrated from the London suburb of Wimbledon and arrived in Canada prior to the First World War. But I was totally unprepared for this lemming-like attitude that intelligent-minded people might be willing to "walk the gangplank" if their English headmistress ordered them to. The "writing on the wall" was steadily becoming more neon-lit for me all the time.

Authoritarianism 101

T his whole situation of small-time "dictators in disguise" being corrupted by the power they yielded reminded me of my college days from almost a decade earlier. At that time, I found myself dealing with an egomaniacal man who had been program head for what seemed like eons. His opening remarks to spirited new students on the first day of classes were always a lesson in demoralization and intimidation.

"Look to the student on your left. Now look to the student on your right. By the end of this semester, one of you will be gone."

Through all sorts of cunning actions on his part, he would spend the next few months ensuring his prophecy was fulfilled.

My natural distrust for authority figures, part of the legacy from having grown up with an alcoholic parent, enabled me to see through his lies and call his bluffs. After finding a female student who shared the same disbeliefs as I did, we organized a group of other like-minded classmates.

While always maintaining there was strength in numbers, our motley crew would gather at her modest apartment for weekend strategy sessions to discuss our next move. We could have been military generals planning our final assault, if not for her penchant for smoking pot and its regular delivery to her front door. Maybe that was the reason these meetings were so well attended.

In the end, we would lead a successful student protest to the college president's office, demanding that action be taken. Apparently, students had been submitting anonymous complaint letters for many years, but to no avail.

Setting aside any desire for axe-grinding vengeance, my personal goal was to seek justice in this matter. This would be achieved the following week in the form of a private and confidential student evaluation of the program. The appropriate "head" would go on to roll fairly quickly after that.

If there were wrongs to be righted in an organization, like a moth being irresistibly drawn to a flame, I would be there. But attempting to return to the task of being a regular student again, now seemed so ordinary. Nothing could match the adrenaline rush of being such a "giant killer." The monotony of my daily classes, combined with a renewed battle with manic-depression, would eventually lead me to dropping out of college altogether. This form of self-destruction was becoming a familiar pattern in my life.

Musical Chairs

B ack on board the HMS Bounty, continuing with my
cross-training, I was now transferred to a more financially
responsible position in the cash cage of the shipboard casino.
Counting stacks of money and sorting valuable poker chips
became my new routine. There were three of us glorified cashiers
working together at all times, with the new kid in the cage
getting the high stool closest to the door.

I didn't recognize the significance of this seating plan,
until one night during a storm at sea. With the ship rocking
from stem to stern and gamblers trading in their chips for
Dramamine motion sickness pills, my fellow cashiers would
take turns yelling my name out when it came time for me to
jump. The heavy metal door to the vault behind me would swing
back and forth with all its might, clearing away anything in its
path, including fresh employees such as myself.

Having finished his shift earlier, Raj would regularly call
me in the cash cage late at night.

"Hey man, when are you coming down to the crew bar?"

I could always recognize his distinctive East Indian accent over the phone, even above the incessant bell ringing of row upon row of slot machines opposite me.

The crew bar was our meeting place; the way many of us civilian sailors dealt with working long hours in such an isolated environment. Offering cheap alcohol, it helped keep restless staff appeased until the end of the next day. This was quickly turning into a nightly "booze cruise."

Bon Voyage

Wherever I went on board, staff members seemed to have heard about my act of defiance concerning Cassandra and had their own private collection of horror stories to share.

I debated rallying the troops, college student-style, for somewhat of a modern-day mutiny. But I soon realized that I would be left alone in such a risky venture, since "talk was cheap" amongst my fellow captives.

My disillusionment with life at sea became too overwhelming to resist any longer. Delivering my resignation halfway through my contract appeared to be the only option left for me.

As I handed in my uniform and bid my farewells on that final day, I had an inkling of how a prisoner must feel when released from their stifling sentence of captivity. Walking down the gangway leading to the pier in Old San Juan, I glanced back at the gleaming white ship behind me one last time. Like the warm gentle breeze blowing off the sea, the idea that God had other plans for my life now swept over me.

Godspeed

G od has given us all free will and the freedom to choose in our individual lives. What paths we venture down and which forks in the road we turn onto, are our decisions to make. Sometimes we are the driver, while other times we find ourselves being the passenger in this lifelong quest.

It was Pierre Teilhard de Chardin, the respected French philosopher-theologian, who said: "We are not human beings on a spiritual journey, but spiritual beings on a human journey." The Bible confirms this insightful perspective. "So we fix our eyes not on what is seen, but on what is unseen, since what is seen is temporary, but what is unseen is eternal." *2 Corinthians 4:18*

Remarkably, the act of faith is quite simple, but with such far-reaching personal ramifications. "Now faith is confidence in what we hope for and assurance about what we do not see." *Hebrews 11:1*

It is indicative of the human spirit that we keep looking forward and moving ahead, in the hope that things will get better, no matter what happens along the way. We aren't here simply as the result of some random act, filling in time and marking off days on a calendar. Thankfully, there is a greater purpose in life planned for each of us. Godspeed.

JOHN HUBERT PEKRUL (JACKIE)
OCTOBER 04, 1961

About the Author

J ackson King is a graduate of Public Relations and Broadcast Journalism. He has worked in diverse positions, including Communications Writer, Information Officer and College Instructor. King is married and lives in Vancouver, British Columbia, Canada.

Front Cover Photo: Walter Marler holding Lloyd, Kenneth, Samuel, Madaline, and Belle holding Price (*circa* 1916)

Back Cover Photo: Madaline King, Hubert King and Dorothy King (*circa* 1940s)

Author Photo: Jackson King at Mirror Lake in Camrose, Alberta, Canada (2015)

CPSIA information can be obtained
at www.ICGtesting.com
Printed in the USA
LVHW04s0411110818
586441LV00001B/1/P